PUBLIC SPEAKING

FOR AUTHORS, CREATIVES
AND OTHER INTROVERTS

Joanna Penn

Public Speaking for Authors, Creatives, and Other Introverts.
Second Edition.

Copyright © Joanna Penn (2014, 2019). All rights reserved.
Publisher: Curl Up Press
www.CurlUpPress.com

For any inquiries regarding this book, please email:
joanna@TheCreativePenn.com

ISBN: 978-1-913321-08-6 (Paperback)
978-1-913321-09-3 (Large Print)
978-1-913321-10-9 (Hardback)

Cover and Interior Design: JD Smith

Printed by Amazon KDP Print

www.CurlUpPress.com

Contents

Part 3: Practicalities of the speaking business 91

Introduction

"Speaking is not an act of extroversion."

Malcolm Gladwell

A few years ago, I spoke to a large group of authors at the London Book Fair about book marketing. During the talk, I mentioned I was an introvert and that one sentence entirely changed the dynamic of the room. I received so much feedback from sharing my story of introversion that I wanted to write this book, to demonstrate that introverts can be professional speakers if they wish, and to teach authors and creatives how to utilize public speaking as part of their business, either as a form of book marketing or to create a separate income stream.

Since then, introversion has become more visible and accepted, in large part due to the success of Susan Cain's fantastic book, *Quiet: The Power of Introverts in a World That Can't Stop Talking.*

> Wherever you are on the continuum of personality types, there's never been a better time to embrace who you really are.

The title of this book comes from my own experience. I'm an author and an introvert, someone who recharges energy by being alone. I'm a creative entrepreneur, making a full-time living from my writing. I'm also a professional speaker, and public speaking is an income stream for me, as well as a distribution method for my books and a marketing tool.

I also love doing it, and that passion is why I want to help you on your own speaking journey.

As creatives in a crowded world, we can no longer sit in our rooms, creating alone, if we want a viable income.

Increasingly, we have to be out there in the world, sharing our knowledge and being visible in order to have a successful career. It's also a good idea to plan for success, and authors/creatives often have to speak when they become well-known, so it's best to start practicing earlier before you really need those skills.

This book is an easy reference guide with the information that you need the most to speak confidently and professionally in public. And, although some chapters have specific tips for introverts, much of this information will be useful for anyone who is interested in public speaking, regardless of personality type.

My story

My career path has been a winding one, which I think is common for many creative entrepreneurs these days!

After doing a Masters degree in Theology at the University of Oxford, I joined Accenture, a global management consulting company. I spent 13 years implementing computer software into large corporates and companies across Europe, Australia and New Zealand. Although I had some fantastic experiences and made great friends, I was never happy in that job, and I felt as if my creativity died a little every day. I tried a number of times to get out, starting a scuba dive charter business, a foray into property investing and other business ventures that ultimately failed.

In 2007, determined to find a path that made me happy as well as solvent, I wrote my first book, *How to Enjoy your Job or Find a New One*, later rewritten and re-released as *Career Change*. That book changed my life as, in the process of writing it, I learned more about myself and what I wanted to do. I also learned about publishing and ultimately about marketing and online business.

At that point, I also decided that I wanted to speak professionally in order to share my story and help others trapped in corporate life.

I joined the National Speaker's Association in Brisbane, Australia, where I was living at the time, in order to learn from professionals. I began speaking for free at local writers' groups and networking meetings and then speaking at professional events, charging for appearances. In 2010, I spoke at a four-day retreat in Bali, and since then I've spoken in London, Zurich and Berlin as well as other cities in Australia, England, and all over the USA. Although I consider myself primarily a writer, with thrillers under the name J.F.Penn and non-fiction books under Joanna Penn, I'm also an international professional speaker, and speaking is now part of my creative business.

When I first started my journey of public speaking, I thought that I had to develop another, separate, persona for the stage. I had spent years in the corporate environment developing an extroverted shell because I thought that the real 'me' wasn't acceptable. I thought I needed to do the same thing as a speaker since the most well-known models were people like Tony Robbins.

But that wasn't the authentic me, and I struggled to find my true voice as a speaker. When I finally embraced my introversion, I was able to develop a sustainable speaking style that both nurtured me and served the audience. I want to help you do the same.

"Appearance is not reality. Some people act
like extroverts, but the effort costs them in energy,
authenticity and even physical health."

Susan Cain, Quiet.

About this book

In this book, I'll share everything that I know as a professional speaker and introvert. It contains lots of tips about public speaking in general, based on my own experience over the last ten years.

In addition, I cover some specific points that creative introverts need to consider as speakers. You can read this book from start to finish, but you can also dip in and out, as each chapter contains tips that you'll need at different times on your journey.

Part 1 goes into the **practicalities of speaking**: types of speaking, preparation, your actual talk, and what happens afterward.

Part 2 is about some of the **psychological aspects** of speaking: your mindset, authenticity, confidence, and tackling the inevitable anxiety, which we all feel.

Part 3 discusses the **business side** of speaking: financials, marketing, and how to create multiple streams of income.

The **Appendices** contain resources that may be useful in your speaking journey. You can also find audio interviews with speakers from the book, as well as accompanying downloads at:

www.TheCreativePenn.com/speakingdownload

Let's get started!

Why speak anyway?

"Most of us realize that at a certain point in your career, whatever you're doing, that it would be advantageous for you to be able to stand up and persuade other people of the value of your ideas and your point of view. **It's going to open a lot of doors that would be closed otherwise.**"

Mark McGuinness, WishfulThinking.co.uk

Why do you want to make speaking part of your portfolio? Here are some possible reasons.

(1) Help and inspire people

One of the most rewarding things about speaking is sharing your message and changing people's lives. If you're passionate about your topic and you communicate well, you will touch individuals, sometimes in unexpected ways. Watching the light dawn in someone's eyes as they suddenly understand that their life can change is fantastic, and I think many of us speak to help others. This is an intrinsic reward and the reason why some people speak for free to groups that might not be able to afford professional speakers otherwise.

Whenever I am exhausted from speaking and traveling and think that perhaps I want to give it all up, this is the anchor I hold on to. I made a commitment when I started my blog, TheCreativePenn.com, in 2008, that I wanted to help release a million books into the world. Every person that I empower to write, publish and market their book adds to the tally, and whenever I speak, I add a few more to the list.

Whatever you speak about, consider how you might change people's lives.

(2) Personal development

Speaking can be personally transformative. When you craft a talk, you have to organize your thoughts into a coherent structure and lead people through a story. This helps to order your own thoughts and can change the way in which you think about a topic. Writing this book has helped me to clarify further what I want from my own speaking career, and we often teach what we need to learn the most.

Going outside your comfort zone is also valuable for personal development, and speaking in front of a crowd is one of those skills that can transform you and give you more confidence.

It can also enable you to face your fears and help yourself by helping others. You will share your own stories and personal experience, and in sharing from your heart, you might be able to work through your own issues.

(3) Market your creative work and harness word-of-mouth

Speaking enables you to connect directly with people, and they are more likely to become fans of your creative work through seeing your face and hearing your voice. If people listen to you and see you in action, they get to know you better. They can ask you questions, and you can demonstrate your knowledge. You connect with individuals this way, and great marketing is best done with a personal connection.

If you give a fantastic talk or seminar, if you are memorable for all the right reasons, people may well talk about you to their friends. This generates word-of-mouth publicity for you — the very best kind. People may buy your books or creative products, or attend your next workshop.

(4) Stand out in a crowded market

Thousands of books and millions of creative products are put on sale each week, so how do you stand out?

Being a professional speaker can help, because most people would rather do practically anything else than speak in public. You have an advantage if you speak because you can say yes to new opportunities which many other authors will turn down.

(5) Successful creatives have to speak eventually

Best-selling authors and creatives speak at festivals, conventions, and events and also appear on the radio, TV, podcasts, and other media. Therefore, if you want to plan for success, you need to prepare for these events and make sure that you fulfill the audience's expectation when you get there.

I've been at plenty of literary festivals where authors have given a poor performance, and it has affected the way in which they are perceived by the audience. In comparison, those authors who can entertain and inspire in person will draw more readers to their written work — and sell more books!

(6) Multiple streams of income

Speakers can earn a good speaking fee for a keynote speech, but can also run workshops or other events that may generate significant income.

Many speakers sell books and products at events, but you can also include the price of a piece of your work in the cover charge so that all attendees get one as part of the event. 'Back of the room' sales are almost guaranteed if you give a great talk or workshop or seminar because people want to take something of you home as a reminder of a great event.

You can even start by speaking on a topic and then turn that into a book later, repurposing your material in several ways. For more detail, check out my book, *How to Write Non-Fiction: Turn Your Knowledge into Words*.

(7) Expenses-paid travel

This may be more of a personal reason, but I'm a travel junkie, and one of my goals around professional speaking is to use it as a vehicle for travel experiences. I may even say 'yes' to speaking at an event because I want to visit the location or say 'no' because I've been there before.

When I speak in different cities or even a different country, I generally stay on for a day or two after the event and experience a new place. This might offset the income goal in many instances, but I often get ideas for my novels when I travel. It is a life priority for me, and it nourishes my creative soul.

(8) Serendipity

You never know who is in the audience when you speak, or what will come from your appearance on a particular day. It may be that someone talks to someone else, and suddenly you get a call that changes everything. You'll never know unless you put yourself out there.

So, what are *your* reasons for speaking? Write them down, because the answers will help you to weigh up the rest of this book.

What is an introvert?

"Introverts are drawn to the inner world of thought and feeling, extroverts to the external life of people and activities. Introverts focus on the meaning they make of the events swirling around them; extroverts plunge into the events themselves. Introverts recharge their batteries by being alone; extroverts need to recharge when they don't socialize enough."

Susan Cain, *Quiet: The Power of Introverts in a World That Won't Stop Talking*

Before we get into the details of public speaking, I wanted to go into more depth around introversion, as understanding some of these things about myself has changed my life.

We're all different, and we all exist on the spectrum of personality. There are no absolutes, and we move up and down the scale, even during the span of a single day. There is no 'better' type of personality and no value judgment as to where you sit.

Introversion doesn't have to define your entire existence, and many people have trouble with labels as if somehow they diminish us. But I find that these labels are tools for understanding an aspect of ourselves and that making the most of our lives is easier when we know ourselves better. It's certainly helped me.

One popular way to see where you sit on the spectrum is to take a Myers Briggs test. There are free options online. It is a blunt tool, but it may be interesting to see your results. I'm INFJ, a common personality type amongst writers, although rare in the general population.

Portrait of an introvert

One of my favorite testimonials from a live event says, "Joanna is the Energizer bunny of writing, publishing and book marketing."

But that quote represents only one aspect of who I am.

I'm an energetic speaker, passionate about my topic. I bring my own bounce, aiming to inspire as well as educate. I am usually vibrating at such a high level by the end of an event that I'm physically shaking, and I'm exhausted afterward. As much as I love it, speaking takes a lot out of me. This used to worry me until I came to understand my own introversion.

Here are some of my introverted personality traits that you might recognize in yourself, or perhaps in those that you know and love.

I enjoy spending time alone. Writing, creating, thinking, reading, and being alone make me happy. I do like being with people, but I need a lot of time alone, and it's how I recharge. If I don't get that alone time regularly, I go a little crazy!

When I'm sociable, **I prefer one-on-one meetings** or small groups, as opposed to large groups or parties which are overwhelming and exhausting.

I don't like small talk. I'd rather ask you about your passions or fears than what was on TV last night. I'd rather say nothing than talk on the surface of life. If I'm being quiet, I'm probably thinking deeply about something else, so please don't be offended. I don't like conflict or arguments, so even if I violently disagree, I'd rather walk away than engage, although I may address it in writing later.

I'm **hyper-sensitive to surroundings and noise.** I find crowds and parties an assault on my brain, battering me into submission. When I do go to parties, I usually drink alcohol and spend a lot of time on the dance-floor. People think I'm the life and soul, but an introvert can be alone while dancing. Now you know all my secrets!

I'm not shy or afraid of new people, but I find networking events difficult, because of the noise and stimulation levels. I used to do a lot of networking events at the beginning of my entrepreneurial career because it seemed the best way to meet people. I have since made many more business contacts and friends by meeting people on Twitter and then having a Skype call one-on-one, which I have found much easier.

[Note: Shy is a different scale in terms of personality. For example, you can be a shy extrovert.]

I hate the telephone. Cold calling, or speaking to people on the phone, is never going to be a way that I can attract business, and I rarely even answer my own phone. I prefer to email and arrange a specific time to talk when I can plan my energy levels.

I'm happy sharing my intimate thoughts and ideas through writing and online and prefer to communicate using the written word or through my podcasts. I have strong opinions and like to express them, but I won't raise my hand to ask a question in a crowded hall.

When I'm tired, I become more introverted, needing to be alone and quiet. If I don't manage my energy well, I can end up having to leave events early. This has happened to me a lot at conferences, especially multi-day events. This is why I choose my speaking events carefully now, making sure it's of benefit to the audience but also taking care of my energy flows.

* * *

If you recognize yourself in any of these points, I highly recommend that you read *Quiet* by Susan Cain, or watch her TED talk on the power of introverts. The book has chapters specifically around the business, educational, and even spiritual dimensions of introversion. *Quiet* helped me to recognize my own personality and begin to embrace truths about myself that I kept hidden for years. When I read *Quiet*, I felt an immense sense of relief as I realized that I'm not a freak, I'm not abnormal, and I no longer have to pretend to be an extrovert in order to be accepted.

This is me, and I have discovered that other people are like me, too. Perhaps you're one of them?

Part 1: Practicalities of speaking

1.1 Types of speaking

There are a number of different types of professional speaking. It's unlikely that you will end up doing all of these, but many speakers incorporate some of them into their businesses for different events.

Keynote or inspirational speaking

Keynote talks are usually short and more about inspiration and entertainment than education. There is often an emotional element that leaves the audience enthused and excited. Keynotes are often given at events or conferences to set the tone at the beginning and end, as well as being given as after-dinner speeches or at special occasions. There is usually no audience participation, interaction, or Q&A.

Content speaking

Content speaking is a broad category that includes longer talks, half-day/full-day/multi-day events, seminars and workshops where the speaker might give one or several longer talks, and the audience is smaller and more involved.

This is my most common type of speaking, and it is about teaching the audience something specific, usually accompanied by slides and handouts. The audience goes away equipped with knowledge to do something and feel empowered with all the practical knowledge that they need, as well as, hopefully, some inspiration.

Workshop presentation or facilitation

Workshops can be a kind of content speaking, but the focus is on the participants doing practical work. Writing workshops are a great example of this, as often the speaker gives a short talk, and then the participants do multiple writing exercises over the day. The main workload is carried by the participants themselves, but the skill of a facilitator ensures that everyone in the room is engaged. The audience numbers for a workshop like this are usually small, with more attention given to individuals.

MC or event Chair

Professional MCs (Master of Ceremonies) manage events, conferences, or special occasions. They keep the ball rolling, introduce other speakers, and often throw in jokes and distract from any issues. This is a specialty job and can be highly paid as, done well, the MC ensures that the event goes off without a hitch. You might think that this sounds like an extrovert role, but I've met a number of comic speakers and professional MCs who align with introversion.

Chair of panel or panelist

Many conferences have panels, and you may be asked to speak as the Chair or as a panelist on a specific topic.

Reading or performing your own work

Literary or creative festivals may ask you to read from your book, or you may go into performance poetry or open mic situations.

All of these types of speaking have their pros and cons, and I'll be going into more detail in the sections to come.

1.2 Deciding on your topic or niche

You cannot be everything to everyone.

You have to decide on your focus, and the more specialized you are, the more successful you are likely to be. You can have multiple offerings around a topic, but, in general, you need to stand out in a specific niche by being perceived as an expert. This is the way to get word-of-mouth recommendations and future work, as people who are in the same industry talk to each other. Here are some tips for working out your niche.

Start with your expertise and your passion

You need to be an expert who speaks. Authenticity and credibility are key, so start from where you are.

What do you know about? Write a list of all the different things that make up your experience. Perhaps you have a book already or years of expertise in a particular field?

Out of that list, what are you passionate to speak about?

It needs to be something that inspires you for the long term.

You also need to decide what makes you unique and how you can stand out from others who speak on the same topics. For example, I write thrillers and non-fiction, but I don't teach live classes on the craft of writing, as that niche is crowded and already well-served. Instead, I focus on creative entrepreneurship which helps me stand out, as very few authors also teach the business side.

Choose a market that people actually want and will pay for

Think about who is interested in your proposed topic, in order to determine whether there's a market.

Who are those people? What do they want? What benefit will they get from your talks? Who already caters to them? For example, is there already a conference circuit for that niche?

You also have to decide what your speaking goal is and how you want your life to look if you are successful.

There are speakers who make a multi-six figure income from speaking events, and if you want that, you need to aim for higher-paying audiences, for example, the corporate market, highly paid keynotes, and audiences who can make money from your advice. You will also need to speak a lot and may have to travel a great deal.

If you're aiming for supplemental income, travel, and personal development from your speaking, then you can consider smaller niches. For example, I speak to writers, authors, and other creatives, mostly self-employed people who don't expect to pay as much as corporates for an event. I'm also an author first, so I don't want to speak full-time. I take on a few key speaking events per year in a highly targeted market.

You get to choose.

Look at speakers' bureaux and what others are doing

Google 'Speaker's Bureau' and browse the categories of what people are speaking on.

For example, corporates pay highly for speakers on Leadership and Peak Performance. Perhaps your expertise fits into that category, but how will you stand out in that particular niche?

Watch other speakers live or on TED.com and then go check out their speaking page to see what their specific niche is and where you might fit.

If you're unsure what your topic is, decide what it's not

This can sometimes take some time as well as trial and error.

When I was unhappy in my day job as a management consultant, I wrote a book for miserable cubicle slaves like me. I initially went down the path of speaking to groups about career change, but it didn't energize me. It felt uncomfortably close to what I used to do as a job, even down to wearing the same pin-stripe suit. So I began speaking to groups of creatives and people starting their own small businesses, and I loved it!

Decide on your message

Once you have decided on your topic, you need to explore that in-depth, expanding on your area of expertise to become super-knowledgeable.

Writing a book is one great way to sort out your own ideas, but one of the most important things to do is to read around the niche so that you get all kinds of other perspectives. There will always be hundreds of books on a popular topic: for example, there are a lot of books on public speaking. But this is my take, based on my experience of being an introvert and a creative, which is quite a different viewpoint. It will be the same for your niche. For more detail, check out my book, *How to Write Non-Fiction.*

Try to make sure that you have a scalable topic. For example, my overarching drive is to empower authors and creatives to be entrepreneurs, and my key message is that anyone can have a successful creative business. That can be an inspiring 30-minute keynote or a five-day workshop with in-depth sessions. You are likely to end up with a few specific topics that you can present on, and you can hone this over time as you get more experience.

1.3 Preparation for the event

Preparation is one of the most important things, especially as a new speaker, regardless of personality type. Here are some of the key areas for preparation before an event.

Talk in detail with the event coordinator or create a questionnaire

The biggest issue you will likely have as a speaker will be a mismatch of expectations, and it may be a disappointing experience for you and the audience if you get this wrong.

You need to know about the audience. Who are they? What do they do? What do they want out of the session? How can you best serve them?

What is the overall theme and goal of the event? What kind of tone is expected?

Agree on a title for the session with the organizer. This may be something you already do or a specifically slanted talk for that particular event. You also need all the specifics around the timing and venue, dress code, and other practical details.

See Appendix 1 for my pre-speaking booking sheet, which includes the questions that you need to consider.

If you're running your own event, you can set expectations through your sales page, but you can also personalize the session further. For my own seminars, I send a questionnaire to the attendees a few weeks prior to the event itself. I use Google Forms, which is free and easy to use.

Try to give people open questions so that you get longer answers, and then integrate their questions and thoughts into your talk. For example, What is your biggest question about X? or What are you struggling with around X?

A questionnaire can also help gauge the level of the audience. For example, I speak about online publishing, book marketing, and creative business, but it is a very different talk if my audience are writing their first book vs. professional authors with 10+ published books and years of experience behind them.

Tailor your material to the specific audience

Most speakers will develop a certain number of presentations, slide decks, and stories that they can deliver to audiences. But it's also important to tailor the material to the specific audience. The more you know about who you're talking to, the more relevant your material will be for them.

I sometimes speak about branding and online marketing. I've given a similar talk to groups of authors, to small business owners like accountants and also to a gaming/ hospitality conference with people who owned pubs and casinos. Although the ideas and principles were the same, and the main slide pack was similar, I used examples that were relevant to each audience, so the presentation was specifically tailored.

When you know your topic in-depth, when the fabric of your message comes from your own life, then you can also anticipate what people will ask you. In my workshops on marketing for creatives, I put up a question on the screen. "What are your feelings about marketing right now?"

Then I open it up to the floor, and people share with the group. Because my talk is based on my own experience, I know what is likely to be said, and in my subsequent slides, I tackle all of those points and over the course of the day, change the perspective of the audience. Consider what questions your topic will raise, then make a list of them and prepare your answers in advance.

Arrive early and prepare the space

In terms of what to bring to the event itself, I've included my speaking checklist in Appendix 2. I pack my bag the night before and recheck the next morning against the list.

If you're speaking at a conference, arrive earlier than your slot. I like to listen to at least a few other speakers beforehand, to get a feeling for the mood of the audience, and it's good to refer back to what they've already said. You'll also need to speak to the organizer and technician to ensure that your slides are cued up and check the microphone arrangements, so make sure to arrive in a break or at lunchtime.

As a female speaker, I often wear dresses. It's best to have pockets for bigger events where you use a microphone as the battery pack needs to go somewhere!

For smaller events, workshops, or your own events, you should arrive early and check all of the arrangements, rearrange the room as you like it and settle in.

If you're ready early, you can be free to chat to people as they enter. I like to do this for a number of reasons.

Firstly, it calms your nerves, because you can engage with individuals whose eyes you can find in the audience later as you speak. It grounds you, because these are real people, not just a sea of faces. You can also ask them why they're here, and it gives you some live material to add in. Chances are that those thoughts are echoed in others throughout the room.

You can also help to connect people; for example, if I find that there are two people who are writing historical fiction, I might introduce them to each other. Being useful and relevant will make it a better event for everyone, and you'll get some great feedback later!

1.4 Managing your energy

Introverts are energized by being alone and quiet, so being with people for extended periods of time can be draining. As a speaker, managing your energy is crucial, and if you can do this effectively, it will enable you to give your best to the audience, and enjoy the event more yourself. Here are some of my energy management techniques.

Make sure that you schedule time before and after your speaking engagement as 'alone time'

This is something I've learned the hard way, after booking too much into my schedule and then crashing for several days, overwhelmed with fatigue and exhaustion.

On one occasion, I was booked to speak at a multi-day conference and was looking forward to spending time learning from others, as well as speaking myself. But I hadn't allowed enough alone time in my schedule and ended up leaving a day early to go and recharge. Now I make sure to have at least a full day either side of speaking with nothing booked in and also restrict my speaking engagements to a couple per year. You'll need to find your own balance, but I recommend using a calendar to block out down-time in advance.

Try to get some time in a full-day session to be alone or have a walk

If you're teaching a full-day workshop, you do need to be available to the audience during the breaks, but try to make sure that you get at least a few minutes when you can be alone. Ideally, this would be a walk outside in the fresh air, but sometimes, for me, it has just been sitting quietly in a separate room, or even in a toilet stall. Anything to close my eyes, breathe, and calm my body.

Carry painkillers for a possible headache

If I don't manage my energy well enough, I will get a migraine and end up in bed for a day or so. You will have your own manifestation of stress and overwhelm, so plan to stop it before it gets too serious.

For more on physical and mental health for creatives, check out my book, *The Healthy Writer*.

Understand your daily rhythms

I'm a morning person, so I tend to do anything social during the day, and I rarely speak in the evenings as that's when I am at my most introverted. You may be the opposite!

It's important to pay attention to your energy levels and identify ways to manage it in order to sustain a healthy relationship with speaking. My worst speaking experiences have come from mismanaging my own energy.

Don't beat yourself up about whatever you need. Just try to anticipate it and schedule appropriate breaks so you can serve the audience and look after yourself.

1.5 Awesome slides. Not death by PowerPoint

I spent 13 years as a business consultant in large corporates, so I know what a slide presentation should NOT be. I've been in those hideous conferences and meetings with tiny fonts and boring speakers droning on for hours. You do not want to be like that!

Why use slides anyway?

You don't need slides to speak. You can give an amazing talk without slides, plenty of people do it, but there are a few reasons why slides are sometimes a good idea:

They allow a **different mode of learning,** and some people need visual input to hang your spoken words on. They can also give another point of focus for your talk, adding depth to your story, and holding people's attention.

Alastair Humphreys, adventurer and speaker, uses his own gorgeous photos from traveling around the world as a backdrop to his message.

"My slides have evolved organically as my talks, and the things that I've done, have gradually evolved. Therefore, the stories I tell evolve … I have a Powerpoint presentation with about 200 slides in, and I pick and choose from those to put together the presentation to fit a specific time … Quite often, I put a quotation from a book or a film that helps to highlight the story and the point that I'm trying to tell."

Alastair Humphreys, adventurer

As a fellow creative, you're likely to have a store of interesting things that you can use as visual aids.

In a workshop or full-day seminar, visual slides can **structure your talk, anchor your message** and help you speak for a longer period without resorting to written notes. It's hard for the audience to concentrate for a full-day session without visuals.

Visuals are **important for showing specific technical information** in a teaching style seminar or workshop. For example, I use slide decks for my full-day workshops on Secrets of Successful Self-Publishing and How to Make a Living with your Writing. As I teach specifics around software and websites for publishing and marketing, I need to show visuals that explain clearly what happens on those sites. I include the slide packs as password-protected downloads so participants can get them from my website later.

The most important thing to remember is that **the slides are not the content, so never read from them**. They should be support for the talk, or for visual effect.

You should also be prepared to speak without slides if the technology goes horribly wrong! I always take a print out of the slides, just in case, as well as a copy on a USB stick.

Make sure that you also check the slides on the technology at the event. I use a Mac, and sometimes you can export to PowerPoint and the fonts resize, plus the resolution can make things go a little wrong. Bigger events may use side screens at different resolutions, and simpler is better when the screens are huge.

Always make friends with the tech team and check your slides at the venue before you go on.

Inspirational and practical resources

I can recommend a few resources to learn about this style of slide presentation.

(1) TED talks have been responsible for the mainstream shift in the way in which slides are used. These short, inspirational talks by individuals with an important message are often accompanied by powerful visuals that give an edge to the words of the speaker.

(2) *Slide:ology* by Nancy Duarte. The Duarte company and this book help people to take their presentations "beyond words and pictures" to become transformative experiences. Check out their portfolio for examples, and the book goes into how to create such presentations yourself. The follow-up book is *Resonate: Present Visual Stories that Transform Audiences.*

(3) *Presentation Zen* by Garr Reynolds. This book and blog use the principles of Japanese minimalist design applied to presentation skills to enhance their impact.

How to create awesome slide packs

Decide on the outcome. Go back to your discussion with the event organizer. What do you want the audience to take away from your talk? What is the emotional tone?

Always focus on the audience and start with what you want them to learn or feel by the end of the session.

Brainstorm the topic and create one slide per key point with one or two words per slide. This helps create a structure. You can, of course, use paper for this, or mind-mapping, or other software. It doesn't matter how you do it, but somehow you need to lead your audience through a journey from beginning to end. I like to use plain white slides in Keynote.

Refine the structure and decide on the **key points, stories, and information** that relate to each slide. I practice what I will say with each slide as I do this, and move them around to organize the narrative flow and journey through the material.

Find images to illustrate each slide. I try to use my own photos where possible. I also use BigStockPhoto.com to buy royalty-free images or use Unsplash.com for Creative Commons images. You can also use Flickr.com Advanced search to find Creative Commons images. Make sure that you reference the creator and link back if you use Creative Commons.

Never download images from a Google search or use other people's images without permission as they are likely to be under copyright.

Populate the slides with images and add any resonant words, phrases, or quotes.

Ensure the order of the slides creates an end-to-end flow. You are leading people through a journey, and they are likely to be at different starting points. I spend a lot of time on the order of my slides, and also add in questions, exercises, and feedback points for longer sessions. As I order the slides, I'm often rehearsing the talk in my head, or even out loud. I never give exactly the same talk twice, even if the topic is the same, and will always update my slide deck for the specific occasion.

Tips for using slides when speaking

Use a handheld wireless clicker so that you can progress the slides without obvious movement. If you're doing talks to bigger audiences, make sure it has a decent range. Many events will have a clicker available for you, but I'd suggest buying your own if you're doing regular events, as well as an adaptor for your laptop to the display. I have turned up at events with my MacBook Pro only to find them missing an appropriate adaptor, but if you have your own, you can just get on with the event with no stress. Mark any devices with your name, so they don't disappear into the conference technology black hole after your talk.

You should be able to see the slides in front of you as you speak without turning away from the audience to look at the screen. I made the mistake at one event of moving too far into the audience, and I couldn't see my slides anymore. I was already nervous and just made it worse by turning around. Don't do this!

When you're speaking with slides, you should **know the transitions** and what's coming next. You can use settings on Keynote to show the next slide as well as the current one, but you should also know your material well enough so that this isn't necessary.

Be very careful about using sound or video within your slides as inevitably something will go wrong and the audience sit there while you fiddle or even call the tech team over. I always use plain slides with no multimedia to avoid potential issues.

1.6 Handouts, workbooks and download page

Attendees at longer events or full-day talks often expect some kind of takeaway or handout. I try to be as minimalist as possible in terms of paper, and I think that people get more from the session if they take their own notes. Here are some options for your event:

Handouts

Printing can add a lot to your costs, so if you're speaking for an organization, send them a PDF in advance so that they can do it for you. This should be a summary, not your entire slide-pack.

You can also ask the organizer in advance if they want you to do handouts. I did several events for The Guardian Masterclasses in London a few years back, and they required handouts for the attendee pack. I produced a two-page summary which also included the link to the download page for the slides.

Download page

I create a download page on my website for every talk I do. I have a WordPress site, so it's easy to create a password protected page using the Privacy settings.

I include a PDF of the full slide-pack and links to any other notes, plus a link to sign up for my Author 2.0 Blueprint. I tell the audience about it in the first few minutes of the event, so they know they don't have to write everything down.

This serves a couple of purposes. It provides extra value to the customer, as they get more resources than they expected. It cuts down or removes, the need for printing, which saves costs and is more environmentally friendly. It also brings the customer to my website, where they might stay a while and engage with more of my content, as well as possibly joining my email list through the Author 2.0 Blueprint. In this way, I can continue the connection over time, and they may buy more of my books and products later.

Workbooks

If you're running a workshop and your topic has a lot of exercises, you could create a printed workbook for every attendee. Make sure you include the costs of printing into your speaker's fee.

You can also sell these as another product if you self-publish. Just add lines or extra space into a larger size print-on-demand template so that people can write answers to the questions posed in the book.

More detail in this video with notes on how to turn your book into a workbook:

www.TheCreativePenn.com/workbook

1.7 Personal presentation

I'm aware of just how controversial this topic can be, so remember: you are in control of how you are perceived, so you get the choice of what to wear when you speak in public.

As with everything in this book, my thoughts are based on my experience and how I feel about presentation, so take and leave what you like!

Presentation counts, so dress for how you want to be perceived

People see you and judge you before you start to speak, and your appearance projects your brand. I go more into this in Part 3, but whether you like it or not, everyone has a brand. It's created by the impressions and the feelings that you evoke in your audience, whether that's through the images on your website, the tone of your writing and what you wear when people see you for the first time.

I've never been much of a shopper and didn't wear makeup when I started speaking. I didn't dress up at all. But after one of my early talks, a woman came up to me.

"I loved your talk," she said. "You have amazing energy, but your casual appearance detracts from the professionalism of your material."

She made some comments about my clothes and lack of makeup. I felt myself wanting to reject her comments out of hand. Why should it matter what I looked like? It seemed shallow and unimportant compared to the message, which she had clearly taken on board and appreciated.

But as I reflected on her words driving home later that evening, I considered the cover of a book. I firmly advocate using a professional designer if you self-publish, because people *do* judge a book by its cover. I concluded that people were judging me by my appearance before I even stepped onto the stage to speak, and that would impact how my talk was perceived.

Later that year, I went to a professional speakers' conference and observed how the top female speakers presented themselves. These women could command five figures for a keynote, and they dressed like they deserved it. Without exception, they were well-groomed with makeup and clothes that projected their professional brand. Their example prompted my trip to the department store to get a lesson in applying makeup, as well as buying some new clothes for speaking. It's the same principle for men, although you might not need the makeup lesson!

Here are some broad suggestions for personal presentation.

Dress to the venue, the occasion, and the audience

When I worked in the corporate world, we were told to dress smarter than the smartest client. I think that advice still stands, and dressing more smartly will give you extra confidence. If you're an after-dinner speaker at a black-tie event, you clearly need to wear formal attire. If you're speaking in a bar downtown, something more casual is fine. If you're doing a writer's retreat in Bali and teaching on the edge of the jungle (as I have done), then a sarong or shorts is completely appropriate, but on a stage in front of hundreds of people in central London, something smarter might be a good idea.

Dress to your brand

When I spoke on career change to corporates a few years back, I used to wear a black pin-stripe suit. It worked with my message and the audience. But now I'm an author and speak mainly to creatives, I wear colorful dresses and funky jewelry because this fits my brand and how I like to portray myself. I also have jackets for more formal occasions, but as I no longer fit the corporate mold, I don't want to dress in a corporate style.

Alastair Humphreys, adventurer and inspirational speaker, wears jeans and a branded t-shirt with #microadventures (the name of one of his books) when he speaks to groups of aspiring explorers. He has a suit for corporate events, but that mix of 'wearable branding' is effective for less formal talks.

Don't let your appearance distract from your message

People shouldn't remember what you were wearing. They should only remember your message. Don't wear something new that itches, or clothes that make you self-conscious.

If you need to be miked up, you'll need a belt or a pocket or something to hang the battery pack off, so make sure that you have something tech support can work with.

I rarely wear heels, but if I do, I wear boots with thick heels so that I'm comfortable, and also have no chance of stumbling, as there are often steps to a stage. The details will be different for every occasion but think about the practicalities before the event. You want to feel at your best when you speak and what you wear does have a bearing on this.

Consider the possibility of film or photography

Act as if you are always on camera, as you may well be with smartphones in every pocket. Many conferences also have roaming photographers and videographers, and if you're one of the speakers, you will be much more on show than the participants.

As an aside, it's always worth trying to get the card of the photographer, because if they get some good shots, you can always purchase them separately for your speaker page or website. Tight patterns or pin-stripes can look weird on video or in pictures, as I have found with one particular jacket, so be careful of those, or test them out beforehand.

1.8 Pre-speaking rituals

In my experience, the 'speaking state' is something I need to shift into. I can do this quickly if someone asks for an impromptu talk, but generally, I have a routine that eases me in, and this is surprisingly common amongst speakers and other performers.

Rituals are just a way to shift yourself into a peak state for whatever you want to achieve. There are no rules, and you will likely develop your own rituals and preparation routine over time.

In the Netflix documentary, *I Am Not Your Guru*, inspirational speaker Tony Robbins demonstrates his ritual, which includes a lot of physical movement like trampolining, and affirmations. He's one of the most successful speakers in the world, so clearly it's not just for the newbies!

My pre-speaking rituals

On the day of the talk, I am always chronically early. I like to arrive at the venue at least 90 minutes prior to my session and then have a coffee in the vicinity once I know where the physical location is.

While having coffee, I write my intentions for the talk in my journal. These are in the form of positive statements, being grateful for the opportunity, and for how well it will go. It's a way to clear my mind of all the other things I could be thinking about and focus on the people I am about to serve. It's my way of stating my intentions for the day, clarifying what I'm about to do, and focusing on the audience rather than my own anxiety.

After writing my intentions, I read my session notes through again. On the walk to the venue, I listen to my speaker playlist of songs. The loud music lifts my energy so that I'm ready to begin. By the time I walk in, I'm good to go.

Here are some other speakers on their pre-event rituals.

Clare Edwards. Brain-Smart.com

"I'm not religious, but I say a little prayer, and the little prayer is around **letting go of the ego**. I just say, "Please let me be the greatest messenger that I can be so that the people hearing my message get what they need to hear." It's not about me."

Mark McGuinness. WishfulThinking.co.uk

"I'm a big believer in rituals. I use them for all sorts of things. I use them for writing, to get myself in the right frame of mind. I certainly use them for speaking.

One of the things I do is when I arrive **I will arrange the room the way I want it to be**. I'll move the chairs around. I'll set up a table with the iPad and slides and my notes, and I'll usually have one flip-chart on the other side, and pens and stuff laid out.

Another thing I do that might sound a bit woo-woo, but really works, is that **I go through a visualization routine** where I imagine opening up the chakras in my body, and then the last thing I do is I really go into present awareness. So I'm really looking, listening, feeling, going into my peripheral vision, which is a really good way to draw introverts out, and **I imagine my presence literally filling the whole room**.

Metaphorically, you need to fill the room. You need to get the sense that if a door opens behind you, you feel it. If somebody walks in up there, you feel it. You're responsible for everyone in the room, and it really does open you out, that you're 300 feet wide.

So once I've gone through all that — and had some coffee — then I'm ready to go."

1.9 Giving the talk

It's not about you.
It's about the audience.

Yes, I keep repeating that, but it's important! Your focus should always be on **serving the needs of the audience,** which will also help to calm any nerves you have.

The very worst talks are the ones that fail to take into account the needs of the people who are listening. I once heard a publisher talk to a group of newbie authors, all of whom wanted to get published. The title of the talk was How to Get Published, but the speaker spent 90% of the talk explaining her own difficulties with the industry and then a few minutes at the end talking about how to double space a manuscript for submission. It was an excruciating experience, and the audience left disappointed.

Timing

Respect the audience, respect other speakers, and never, ever go over your allotted time. Either finish on time or early, and this is doubly important if there is a break or food involved. You are never more important than food or alcohol!

If you're running your own event, be sure to introduce an agenda so that people know when the refreshment breaks are, and make sure that there are enough of them. If you're speaking at a conference, and the speaker before you has gone on too long, then cut your talk shorter or at least ask the organizer what they would like you to do.

Don't be boring

Speaking should have a healthy dose of passion, and I don't believe that we can be effective without it. Your passion for your topic should come across in your delivery, even if you have spoken on it many times before. If your material is serious or dry, you can still deliver it with energy.

Your body is an instrument

As an author, I spend a lot of time at my desk. I often sit on a Swiss ball and work at a stand/sit desk, which is fantastic for preventing and alleviating back pain, but I still have the posture of a writer.

When I speak, I have to consciously straighten my spine, pull my shoulders back, and stand tall. Posture helps with confidence as well as conveying a strong physical presence in the room.

Being comfortable with your body and being seen is critical in a speaker.

I did a training course nearly ten years ago now, and one of the exercises involved just standing up in front of the group and being looked at for several minutes, without speaking.

The feeling of being watched is something that you need to get used to, and the only way to do that is to experience it. As a speaker, there's a moment when the eyes of the people in the room fall on you.

Embrace it, don't shrink away.

Breathe.

You can get the attention of an audience just by standing silently, no need to hush them.

Your presence can be powerful, so practice standing tall, aware of your physicality.

Self-awareness

In the early stages of your speaking career, it can sometimes feel as if you've just given your talk without being fully present. It's a bit like driving when you know the journey, you do it without thinking or really being aware during the process. Part of this is nerves, but in my experience, the self-awareness develops over time, when you are more confident in your material and your own ability. You can foster it by trying to pay attention to specific things each time you speak, for example, your breathing. This awareness will help you adapt in the moment to the needs and energy of the audience. It just takes practice.

Body movement

Grounding your posture with feet spread and a strong core can help you center and speak with authority, but many speakers will move around a stage, rather than standing in one place or behind a lectern. Either is fine, and you will have to adapt to the venue and the microphone.

Some speakers talk with their hands. I'm a very energetic speaker and find that I am physically drained after speaking for a full day. I bounce, I gesticulate. I can't help it, as I am passionate about my topic, and it can't help but come out physically. You will have your own natural style, which can also be improved by training and experience over time.

Technical aspects

If you move a lot and you have to wear a microphone, ask the sound technician beforehand where the danger spots on the stage are. If you get too close to the speakers, you may get feedback, that horrific noise that destroys the atmosphere of a room.

Be aware of your physical movements and the impact on the audience as well as the technical possibilities.

Make eye contact and use the reactions of the audience to help you pace and moderate the talk

Even with a very large audience, you can make eye contact with a few people, and if you do that within each segment of the room, most will feel that there is some kind of connection with you.

"Look at the audience rather than just looking behind you at the screen … Look at all of the parts of the room, front, back, and get eye contact with as many people as you can. It's essential."

Alastair Humphreys, adventurer

In smaller groups and workshops where you can change tack more easily, use the questions and reactions of the group as you go along to help you craft a more compelling talk, and provide the most value.

Your voice

There are a number of things to consider about your voice, but it often comes back to "don't be boring" and also being aware of the audience reaction.

Speaking is an interactive experience, and you will get feedback from the audience if you watch and listen. Positive eye contact, note taking, and nodding mean that things are going well; confused looks or drooping eyes can indicate that something is wrong. Here are some more specifics around voice.

Volume

The venue and size of the audience will dictate whether a microphone is used or needed.

If the event is being recorded, a mic will always be used. Don't be afraid of asking the technician questions, especially if you're new to this. It's important to get used to the mic rather than be afraid of it.

If there's no mic and there are more than 30 people in a room, it's worth projecting a little (not shouting). Authors, especially, can be a little quiet, so it's best to err on the louder side and look for feedback in the room. People will usually cup their ears at the back before they actually say that they can't hear you.

Pitch and tone

Be sure to vary your tone, because there's nothing worse than a monotone delivery. Even if the topic is life-saving information, people won't listen. They will tune out within seconds.

If you're concerned about this, record yourself speaking. I think that most monotone speeches result from reading text aloud, rather than performing the text, or speaking with slides or notes in a more relaxed manner.

Word choice and metaphor

It's important to adjust your words to the audience and not use slang that only people in your niche understand, for example, the term 'indie author' is commonly used amongst independent authors but those outside the niche still use the term 'self-publishing.'

You also need to be aware of using too many filler words, like 'um' or 'so' and other needless words that don't add to your talk. Use silence for these beats instead.

Use of coarser language will be related to your personal brand and the particular audience. Whatever words you use, actively choose them for the occasion.

Accents

If you're going to be a professional speaker, and you're not speaking in your native language, you have to be really honest about your accent and how well you're going to be understood by your audience.

Accents can be positive, as people love to hear an interesting voice from another culture. But, I've also been at conferences where people have understood very little of what the speaker said, but were too polite to give feedback. That person may wonder why they didn't get booked again.

Silence and pauses

Time feels different when you speak. A second of silence feels like an eternity to you, but to the audience, it's likely to be a necessary moment of reflection. Slower speaking with more pauses is more authoritative. This is something that I personally continue to work on, but it is very powerful if you can master the technique.

If you **pause after an important statement**, you provide gravitas to what you just said. It indicates that you made a critical point, and gives people a chance to reflect or make notes. It can also help you, as the speaker, decide what to say next.

You can **count in your head or take a slow breath in and out**. Take a sip of water or change slides.

Silence can also be useful for nerves. If you're in the middle of speaking, and you forget what you're saying, don't worry. Stop, be silent, and the next thing will come to you, rather than being flustered and running to check your notes.

Trust that your brain contains everything you need. Doing some improvisation training can help with this, and it is something that I intend to do myself, as it also teaches spontaneity and trust in your own creativity.

Breathing

Breathing helps you control the tendency to speak too fast. It calms the nerves and modulates your voice. I have to be consciously aware of my breathing, as sometimes I hold my breath, which speeds up my speaking.

So, keep breathing!

The talk itself

If you're being introduced by someone else, provide a short, written intro by email and also bring a print copy so that they can read from it directly. Your credentials are important as social proof, and it's always great to have someone else list them.

If you're introduced by name, you don't need to re-introduce yourself, but can jump straight into the meat of the talk. Otherwise, **briefly say who you are** and then get into it. Once again, the focus should be on serving the audience, not on you.

Emotional resonance helps people connect to your message, so the overall arc of your talk should be a story or journey, as well as including smaller stories within it. One of my key stories is how I spent years as an IT consultant thinking that I wasn't creative, and how I transitioned into writing fiction. Mine your life for interesting personal details that illustrate aspects of your talk.

Use humor, but that doesn't mean that you should tell jokes. Adventurer and speaker, Alastair Humphreys, uses self-deprecating humor in his talks, and I often use the same technique. You can make people laugh with life situations and stories, but not by Googling the joke of the day. Laughing at yourself, being humble and authentic goes a long way with any audience.

If possible, **leave room for Q&A,** as often people have questions that will be vastly different to what you were expecting, and it can make the talk much more interactive. I try to do this with smaller groups or longer talks but also ensure that I set the scene at the beginning, explaining that we need to keep to time.

Arrive early and stay late. If you chat to the audience

beforehand, it can really help in the talk and give you specific friendly faces to make eye contact with. Always stay until everybody's questions have been answered, even if you have to chat afterward.

Speakers who rush off can be considered disrespectful by the audience, and you'll never know what might have happened if you stuck around to connect. However, as an introvert, I have left early on occasion when my energy levels have dropped so low that I would be useless around people. You need to find a balance.

The end of your talk

Speaking is about leading the audience through a journey of transformation. There should be a flow of emotional and mental states while you have their attention. If you're a motivational speaker, you will be aiming to inspire, uplift, and change people's lives. If you're a content speaker, you'll be instructing and educating, as well as inspiring. The end of the talk is important, as how you finish will determine the energy state that the audience leaves in and how they remember the session.

There are various ways of doing this:

- Finish a story or close a loop that you opened at the beginning of the talk.

- Ask a question or pose a challenge that the audience needs to respond to. This is a call to action.

- Use a quote or an image on the screen that evokes the emotion you want to end with.

I often leave a beat of silence after my ending, so that people know it's over, and then I thank the audience. People usually applaud at this point. Try and accept this thanks with good grace!

In my own workshops, I will then change to a slide with my contact details and the access page for downloading the extra material.

Beware the inspirational montage to music, or anything that involves a change of technology or shift in attention. There is great potential for this to go wrong. Brain-Smart speaker, Clare Edwards, talks about one event where her slide montage played to deathly silence instead of inspirational music.

If you have the attention of the audience, don't shift their attention to something else, but instead, leave them with your final thought.

Giving everything

It's OK to be exhausted afterward. I used to think that my exhaustion at the end of speaking was a failure on my part to manage my energy. But in talking to other speakers about their similar experiences, I've realized that it is just about giving everything to the audience, and that's important.

You have an opportunity to change lives. There are people who will listen to a talk and take action from your speech, who would never read your book or find the information another way. If you've got loads of energy left at the end of your talk, perhaps you haven't given enough.

1.10 Managing people

The amount of interaction that you have with people will depend on your type of speaking and the events you do. I speak mainly during the day, doing seminars and workshops with people who have chosen to be there, so my audience is generally respectful and eager to learn.

The types of people I generally have to actively manage are people who might not know when to shut up or people who want to make the session all about them or turn the conversation to their personal issues. As another example, if you're delivering a keynote after dinner, or you do MC work, you may have to deal with drunk people or hecklers who think that it's funny to interrupt you. All of these take management.

Here are some techniques that you can use for people management in all situations:

Set guidelines upfront

In a workshop or seminar situation where you are in charge of the whole day, you can set guidelines in order to set the tone and expectations of behavior.

I have a slide that I talk about upfront, which suggests we take personal discussions offline and talk about them during the break if the main topic starts to be derailed. I also mention that although I'm happy to take questions and interactions during the talk, I will also move people on if we're running out of time.

Clare Edwards, professional speaker and facilitator at Brain-smart.com, asks participants to make their own rules on how to deal with quiet people (dormice) or those who might like the sound of their own voice (parrots). She gets permission to use a codeword or phrase that can be used to politely move the session on, for example, 'Thank you for your input,' which everyone agrees upfront means shut up.

Always remember that you, as the speaker, are in a perceived position of power

Even if you are feeling attacked by someone else, don't react in a way that belittles the other person. Mark McGuinness talks about empathizing with angry participants, who are often reacting to stress outside the situation. Alastair Humphreys uses humor to dispel any conflict.

I always suggest that we **take the conversation offline** and follow up during the break, or afterward. However you deal with difficult people, it's important to keep the rest of the audience on your side. As an example of how this can shift, I attended a panel at a literary festival one summer, and an audience member took offense at something one of the authors had said. When this man first spoke, I was on the side of the panel, and I agreed with their points. But then the four of them proceeded to lambast him from a physically higher position, as well as being perceived as more powerful. Within minutes, I was angry at the panel for treating a member of the audience this way. There were over five hundred people in the room, and I'm sure that I wasn't the only one whose sympathies shifted.

Use interaction as much as possible in longer talks

Encourage comments and questions from the audience. You can also anticipate their issues and get them to vocalize them. For example, I know that when I talk to creative people about marketing, they will often ask, "How do I balance my time?" I have the material to answer it, but they feel more included in the process if they ask first rather than me just telling them.

Allow introverts in the audience to be quiet

Allow non-interaction without picking on people and enable the audience to join in on their own terms. Extroverts in the room will naturally join in more easily!

When I'm a participant, I hate being asked to share, and I particularly hate sitting in a circle, being forced to say something at the end of a session. Think about how you like to be treated and then be sure to respect your audience in the same way, as you'll always have a mix of personality types in the room.

Social media, photos, and device usage

Only a few years ago, it was considered rude for people to use a computer, tablet, or phone during a talk. Some speakers still insist on no devices.

But we are now a hyper-connected community and many people in the audience will take notes on a device, as well as sharing quotes on social media or monitoring the backchannel of the conference on Twitter.

Yes, they may also be playing a game or checking their

email, but it's not up to you to police their choices. Your job is not to tell them to turn off their devices. It is to be so interesting that they lift their heads to listen more carefully. You are competing with a myriad of other potential distractions, and I find this to be a positive challenge.

Of course, it's best to tell people to turn their phones to silent, but then I actively encourage photos, social media sharing, and selfies after the session.

I include my twitter handle on my slides and include the conference #tag if there is one (and these days, there usually is). I check tweets afterward, responding, and joining in the conversation.

This type of interaction can take the connection onwards and spread your message further through social media marketing. You can even take screen prints of positive social media mentions for your testimonials page.

1.11 Panels

I've been to a lot of conferences over the last ten years of being an author, and I find most panels frustrating. They often seem to be a way to get as many contributors into one session as possible, but no one gets a chance to speak for long, so the conversation stays at a surface level. Too often, one voice dominates, and the audience can leave disappointed.

I've also been a participant on a number of panels, and my experience has varied depending on the others involved, and particularly, the expertise of the Chair in handling the various panel members.

So what happens if you're on a panel, either as a participant or the Chair?

If you're the Chair

Research the members of the panel carefully, understand their likely positions and, if necessary, sound them out beforehand. You need to stay on topic, or the audience will go away disappointed.

Try to ask questions that will draw out new information from the panelists, not the same old, same old that they have talked about before.

Remember **the panel is not usually about you**, the Chair, it's about the members. Introduce yourself, for sure, but keep throwing the conversation back to them.

Introduce the panelists with a brief one-liner and then get into the questions. Too often, the intros can go on for a good chunk of the session if the panel has a lot of people.

Control any participant that dominates, goes off-topic or decides to start self-promoting. A good Chair has to stay on top of behavior like this, as there's not enough time for grandstanding.

Keep the conversation flowing at a decent pace. You don't have time to relax on a good panel.

Don't use (or allow) slides or supporting material, unless they are physical props such as books or creative work. There's no time for potential technical issues with panels.

Leave some time for audience questions but have more prepared just in case there is silence when you ask.

If you're a panelist

Research the Chair and other panelists in advance, so you know their positions on the topic. Decide if there is anyone you particularly want to connect with. Get to know the other panelists in the Green Room beforehand.

Keep your answers short and to the point of the panel discussion. Don't use the time as your personal soapbox. Don't self-promote. If you're interesting and engaging, people will find out about you, and your details are likely to be in the program anyway.

Try to make it interesting for the audience by bringing different points of view. A panel that only has one opinion is boring, although an argument for the sake of it should also be avoided.

If other speakers on the panel are grandstanding, **remain focused on delivering value** in your answers. You will stand out in comparison, and people are likely to remember your professionalism.

1.12 Feedback and testimonials

When you're first starting out as a speaker, you want as much feedback as possible in order to improve your performance. You also need testimonials or recommendations to use on your website and marketing materials. These are quotes from people in the audience or the organizer that act as evidence of your speaking ability.

Don't trust your own emotion

At the end of a speaking session, you may evaluate yourself and come up wanting. But I've learned that although you may feel it went badly, you'll probably get emails and feedback afterward demonstrating that people learned a lot and were touched by your talk.

Also, if you have predominantly introverts in the audience, you may feel people didn't enjoy it much because they were quiet, but you're likely to get emails and social media comments later saying how great it was. That's just the preferred method of sharing for introverts.

So, don't rely on how you think it went. Wait for feedback.

How to get feedback and testimonals

When running my own events, I use a simple written form at the end of the session. The form has two sections: what did you enjoy/what did you learn (testimonial) and then what could be improved (feedback). Alternatively, you could email a feedback form using something like Google Forms, which is free.

For bigger events when you don't have access to the audience directly, you can email the event organizer and ask for a testimonial later.

For testimonials, remember to get permission to use them on your website. I include a checkbox to opt-out of public use on the feedback form. If I get nice emails afterward, I'll often ask for permission to use the comments. If comments are posted on social media, they are already public, so you don't need permission to screenprint those.

If you want specific feedback on your speaking skills, then the best way is to video your performance and analyze it or pay for a professional speaking coach.

You could also ask a fellow professional speaker to attend your event and take notes, and offer to do the same for them. This kind of buddy bartering works well at any stage of your career.

Using feedback

Testimonials help the sales and marketing process, whereas feedback is for you personally, to improve your speaking. You need both to be effective over the long term.

With feedback, just wait a couple of days before reading it as you have asked for honest comments, so some may be negative. Often those same people give great testimonials, so critical feedback doesn't mean that you were totally terrible!

You also need to evaluate what is useful and what is just normal for an event. For example, in my full-day seminars, I will teach the principles of internet marketing. The audience will often be quite diverse; some people will already blog and tweet and watch YouTube; others will be completely confused and not have a clue about any of this. Some of those people will write in their feedback that I went too fast, but others will say that it wasn't granular enough.

Evaluate the feedback as best you can in order to improve your speaking, but remember that you will never please everybody.

Using testimonials

Use specific quotes to add to your speaker web page and also potentially on a longer Testimonials page on your website. This acts as social proof for anyone looking to hire you. You can also use quotes on your marketing material, business cards, and anything else that will encourage people to book you in the future.

1.13 Performing your creative work

Performance of a written work can be a key part of speaking for authors, poets and other creatives. This chapter is written by Dan Holloway, novelist, performance poet, spoken word artist, and fellow introvert. Personally, this type of performance scares me silly, but it is also something to which I aspire, so I wanted Dan to share in more detail.

* * *

Nothing cements your story, and you, in someone's mind quite so much as hearing it straight from your mouth, read with every ounce of the passion that drove you to write it in the first place.

That love for your story as you read from it and talk about it is what makes all those lights of connection go off in a reader's head that mean not only do they feel that they must have this book, but they must read it, and they must tell everyone they know about it.

Now, OK, that "with every ounce of the passion that drove you to write it" bit is something that sends many writers scurrying for the nearest curtain to hide behind. But that's the bit that I hope I can help you with. I'm an introvert. Put me in a party, and I will run for the corner and surround myself with an aura of "don't come near me" until the whole sorry experience is over. But, even though I still go through a cycle of overwhelming nerves before any kind of reading, I have both learned to manage and direct those into my performance, and have come to love being in front of an audience more than pretty much anything else in my creative life.

I want to look briefly at three sets of considerations that I hope will help you to give readings that you love and through which you gain readers who will stick with you for life.

What kind of reading?

Not everyone is suited to the same kind of reading. You need to read somewhere that's suitable both for you personally and for the kind of book that you have. Fortunately, there are more kinds of reading springing up than ever. Of course, the staple remains bookshops, libraries, and schools. But for those of you who write genre fiction, probably the best places for you to approach are conferences and festivals specializing in your genre.

There is also an increase in spoken word performance nights that embrace prose as well as poetry. The trail is being blazed by events like Literary Death Match, Book Slam, Grit Lit, and Short Stories Aloud but reaches down through all levels to the open mic nights that run in almost every town. In fact, I would wholeheartedly recommend anyone to begin with an open mic night. You will get used to the mechanics of reading to an audience, you may well make some new fans, but the spotlight won't be on you. If you can't find something suitable, don't be afraid to approach a venue and ask to set up your own event. That's how I started, with a pleasant conversation with my local bookstore, politely asking if I could hold something there.

Within weeks, I started approaching galleries and cafes, two months later I was standing on stage at Rough Trade Records in Brick Lane, and less than six months after my first reading I somehow wound up in front of more than 100 people in Shoreditch winning Literary Death Match. The door for readings, in other words, is as open as you want it to be.

What do I read?

Now, I started off by saying that the best thing about readings is making an audience fall in love with your book. This is where I go back on that a little. One of the best literary events is Short Stories Aloud. Each event features two well-known authors who write a short story which is then read to the audience by a professional actor. It works wonderfully, even though the writers are usually novelists.

The reason is that the very best reading will do three things:

- hold the audience's attention from start to finish

- make the audience desperate for more

- showcase all of your talents

The inconvenient truth is that very few passages from a novel will do all three, or even two, of those.

A great reading, to do all of these should:

- **Be short**. Eight minutes is the longest you can possibly keep an audience rapt. Five minutes is about right for prose. You can, of course, do more than one five-minute piece during an evening.

- **Show all of your talents.** However experimental your style, the best readings have a clear narrative arc and will demonstrate your skills at pacing, description, and dialogue.

A short story will usually accomplish these better than a novel excerpt.

What do I do?

So, you have a reading lined up, and you know what you'll read. You have the right audience and the right material, so how do you ensure that they will come away inspired and wanting to be a lifelong fan?

The best piece of advice that I was ever given came from a writer friend who's also a professional actor. She told me, **"figure out in advance what to do with your spare hand."**

The following tips will help you to perform to the very best of your ability:

Rehearse. Lots. And then more.

Go to the venue in advance. Stand or sit where you'll be standing or sitting for the reading. Get to know the layout of the room, so you feel comfortable there.

When you do that, **pick an object in the room**, close to where the audience will be, to read to. That way, you won't be distracted by not knowing where to look.

Figure out in advance what to do with your spare hand. Holding a book in one hand really is distracting in a way that you won't realize until you get there and feel this thing waving around by your side. Practice an action, hold something, even put it in your pocket, but plan what you'll do.

Learn to breathe from your diaphragm, and learn breath control so that you only ever have to breathe on the commas and full stops.

If you only invest in one thing, make it an **acting lesson**.

Don't worry if you're nervous. You will be. You certainly should be. That's because you care and want to give your audience a fabulous time. If you have done all of the above, you will have maximized your chance of being able to work through the nerves and channel them into giving a great performance. This is why you need to do all these things in advance (and especially learn your breath control) because when they confront a nervous you, they can send your mind in a hundred directions. If you know the space and are comfortable with your actions and your material, that won't happen.

Practical tips

Ensure that you have **water**. Ask the venue, but bring your own in case.

Always have **cards/bookmarks** with you for those new fans.

Bring enough books, and check the sales arrangements with the venue. Bookstores may want to check your books in as stock and then take their discount. That, after all, is how they make their living, and doing what the venue likes is courteous and the key to a long-term relationship.

Bring a piece of paper for your **mailing list** and actively pass it around the audience.

Have a friend in the audience that you trust to be honest to give you **feedback** and ideally to film you so that you can learn for next time.

Most of all, enjoy it.

* * *

Dan Holloway is a novelist, award-winning performance poet, and creative thinking consultant at www. RogueInterrobang.com

1.14 Improving your speaking

There are four stages of competence when you learn any skill, as described by psychologist Abraham Maslow:

Unconscious incompetence. You don't know what you don't know. In speaking, this might be your first talk, and you just winged it without any knowledge of what you need to learn.

Conscious incompetence. You know what you don't know. Hopefully, this book will start to change those don't knows into knows!

Conscious competence. You know what to do to improve, and you have to actively make sure you use those skills and techniques. For example, I am still at this level with breathing. I have to actively breathe more deeply, or I find myself holding my breath.

Unconscious competence. The skills and techniques are internalized, and you don't have to actively recall them, for example, eye contact with the audience is part of how I speak naturally now. I don't have to think about it; I just do it.

So how do you improve at public speaking?

(1) Speak more

As with any skill, the more you do it, the better you will become.

I had been speaking in my day job for years in corporate workshops, training sessions, and conferences, so when I started speaking professionally, I went straight to speaking for groups, volunteering for networking breakfasts and other free opportunities. Then I did my first paid public workshop and progressed from there. It doesn't matter how you get speaking hours under your belt; you just need to get them.

Whatever you do, reflect on the session afterward and write down what went well and what you think you could improve.

Even if you think it didn't go well, there will likely be some people in the audience who were positively affected by what you said. This is something I've learned over time, and it's a kind of magic! It must be something about connecting as people and sharing honestly, but even when I think a session went terribly, I've received some amazing feedback or an email later saying thank you.

So be conscious of what you can improve, but also don't be too hard on yourself. If you focus on serving the audience, you can't go too far wrong.

(2) Reflect on feedback

As previously outlined in chapter 1.12, I create feedback forms for many of my own workshops and ask for comments from the audience and the organizer. If you collate those responses and assess them over time, you will be able to identify what to improve.

(3) Join a professional organization

Many people start at Toastmasters, which has chapters all over the world, and I highly recommend it if you like structured group activities. I did try a Toastmasters group, but it didn't gel with me personally.

Toastmasters is great if you want to improve at an amateur level, but for me, joining the National Speakers' Association in Australia was key in taking my speaking to the next level. There are associations around the world as part of the Global Speakers' Federation, so you may be able to find a chapter near you from their site.

If you want to be a professional speaker, I'd suggest learning from a professional organization as they teach the business side as well as the craft. Being surrounded by the best speakers in the world at conventions, as well as attending classes on everything from microphone mechanics to pricing helped me progress to paid speaking quickly. If you want to charge for your speaking work, then joining a professional organization will help, because you're surrounded by people who are making money speaking and you'll be part of a supportive peer network.

(4) Go on courses, work with peers or get a coach

You can also get 1:1 professional speaking training or attend a specific course to improve.

I started early by attending a speaking course run by actors for my 18th birthday, and have taken a number of courses since then, including the National Speaker's Association Academy and a course on speaking like a TED-talker.

I intend to do an improv course at some point, and perhaps one on stand-up comedy as I definitely find that aspect more difficult. There's always room for improvement, and I find that professional training is a great return on investment, but then I'm also a learning junkie! I definitely recommend training, but, as with any skill, you do need to actually perform in order to improve. So at some point, stop learning, and get speaking.

You could also find a speaking buddy who is at the same level as you and give each other feedback, preferably by attending each other's talks rather than practicing without an audience, as the energy is quite different. Videoing yourself speaking and then assessing that video with another speaker or coach can also be an excellent way to become more conscious of elements of your performance.

(5) Watch other speakers and take notes

You can watch speakers live, or you can watch a lot of them on YouTube. I recommend starting with TED.com for inspirational speakers. Top-rate comedians are worth watching as well as they have worked an incredible number of hours to get where they are, and their sense of timing reflects this. They also deal with the most challenging audiences and know how to get an emotional reaction.

I find that attending professional organization events really helps me learn new things. When I listen to a speaker, I split my notepad and keep two sets of written notes, half on the content and the other half on the speaking presentation itself. Even if you don't find the session content useful, you can always learn new speaking and presentation tips.

Part 2: Mindset

2.1 Tackling anxiety

"We don't want to get rid of the nerves. We don't want to get rid of the butterflies. There's an old speaker's saying: We want to get them flying in formation."

Clare Edwards, Brain-smart.com

Many people are afraid of speaking in public. It's a totally natural and common fear, so it's very likely that you're going to feel some anxiety symptoms when you speak. These may never dissipate completely and, in fact, you may not even want them to. But before we go any further, think about your conclusions from the beginning of the book. Why do you want to speak? And is it worth tackling these temporary feelings?

Here's a personal example of desire overcoming deep-seated anxiety.

Back in 2000, I left London and went to Western Australia. I learned to scuba dive on the edge of the Indian Ocean, but before I could get into that blue sea, I had to challenge my very real fear of breathing underwater. One of the tests that you have to pass before getting your Open Water certificate is to take off your mask underwater, then put it back on, clear the water out, then take the regulator out of your mouth and put it back again. Yes, you actually have to take the air away from your mouth!

I still remember the anxiety of those moments, heart thumping, brain screaming that I would die. But I wanted what came afterward. I wanted the freedom to swim in the blue, to float over the coral landscape, to move in a new world. I wanted that future so much that I tackled the fear and took the regulator out of my mouth, and later, removed the mask from my face. The actual event wasn't that big a deal in the end, but the fear is greatest BEFORE we attempt something. I still feel nervous before descending to a new dive site, in the same way that I still feel nervous before I speak, but it's worth it. Let's go deeper into this topic.

Why are you afraid?

The most common fears around public speaking are fear of embarrassment, making a mistake and looking stupid; fear of judgment, what people might think of you; and fear of rejection, a primal feeling based on the need to be accepted by a social group.

All of these are completely normal and if you have any more fears, try to identify those, too.

What does anxiety feel like?

Warning: Bodily functions ahead!

I was about to speak to over 300 people in a new venue, and there were some people in the audience that I wanted to impress. Ten minutes before my talk, I went to the bathroom for the third time, my stomach churning. I took a couple of painkillers to stop my stress headache getting worse. I sprayed on extra deodorant as I was sweating more than is considered lady-like. My mouth was dry, so I kept sipping water, exacerbating the need for the bathroom. My heart pounded in my chest as I touched up my makeup unnecessarily.

I took some deep breaths and walked back to the room, singing in my head to psych myself up. I smiled and walked up on stage, and within ten seconds, I had relaxed into my material, my anxiety forgotten.

My fear around speaking has decreased over time, but there will always be occasions it manifests. Here are some common physical symptoms you might experience:

- Stomach pain, nausea, diarrhea, and frequent urination

- Excess sweating

- Heart thumping and pulse pounding; vision may narrow

- Headache, feeling faint, shortness of breath

This is all normal!

Nowadays, I recognize these 'symptoms', and, like any anxiety, there are ways to manage it. The moment I stand in front of an audience, the second I am seen, I become "Joanna, the speaker." When I start speaking, the anxiety disappears, and I love the experience. Like my scuba diving example, the fear is worse than the actual event.

But some anxiety is a reality, and if you want to speak, you have to find ways to deal with it. Here are some of my tips:

Reframe the experience

It's not about you, it's about the audience, and they're only interested in what they can learn from your talk. So if you speak in the spirit of serving the audience, it can reduce your own fear.

Acknowledge your anxiety, accept it without judgment, and reframe the event from a place of service.

Embrace and use the energy

Robert Rabbin, a fantastic speaker and teacher, once taught me that anxiety can be perceived as 'shakti,' creative energy that we actually *need* to speak. It gives us that extra edge, that hyper-awareness, a buzz that we can communicate to the audience as we speak. Without it, we may be dull and uninspiring.

Be incredibly prepared

I talked about preparation in more detail in Part 1, and I definitely recommend that you use written notes or a slide presentation for your first speaking engagement. If you understand who the audience are and what they want, and you've prepared something that will inspire, entertain, or educate them, you'll be fine.

Meet some people in the audience earlier on

This is hard for introverts, as you have to approach strangers, but I will often introduce myself as one of the speakers and ask people why they're at the event. I can then tailor my stories more specifically to them or find out some tidbit that helps me to ground the talk in real life. People are people, like you and I. Those in the audience are generally on your side, keen to listen and learn, and they don't want you to fail. If you can make eye contact with some friendly faces, it will help.

Do some visualization and/or breathing exercises

Long, slow, deep breaths can calm a fast-beating heart and help to slow your whizzing brain.

In for four, out for four.

Use music to help you change states

I have a playlist that I listen to on my way to the speaking venue. It's usually loud music with a strong beat and empowering words that gets me into the right headspace to be the best speaker I can be and give my all to the audience, even if I don't feel like it.

* * *

In the end, you have to accept that anxiety is part of the speaker's experience. Everyone has it to a lesser or greater extent, so understand that it's not unusual and work out ways to channel it. Focus on why you're speaking and the needs of the audience, and it will become easier over time.

2.2 Growing your confidence

Confidence is a belief in your own competence and your ability to deliver on your promise to the audience. Confidence as a speaker comes from:

Expertise and deep knowledge of your topic

If you know your material inside out, you will have a deep well of confidence to draw on.

Preparation

Knowing the audience, context, and the practicalities of your talk will specifically anchor your preparation. Having your slides printed out as well as on a USB key and emailed to yourself will give you confidence that if anything happens, you're prepared. If all the technology fails, you can still talk to an audience with written notes.

Authenticity

No one can challenge who you are or your real-life stories. No one can take those away from you. If you speak from an authentic place, then you can be confident because of your personal experience. Even if there are many other speakers who talk on the same topic, you will still bring your original take.

Confidence is a choice

A speaker is in a position of authority, so you need to project confidence, even if it is a quiet form. There's a little bit of 'fake it until you make it' at the beginning, but if you remember that you're in service to the audience, that will see you through.

Never apologize on stage, for example, "I'm sorry I'm so nervous." That is the mark of someone focused on themselves. Remember that no one cares about you; they just want to know how you can help them. Project confidence, even if you're not feeling it inside.

Understand that you will never be perfect, and don't beat yourself up about it

There may be the rare occasions when everything goes amazingly well — when every single person in the room is engaged, when you are amazing, the technology works, you feel fantastic, and everyone's lives are changed. That's just not going to happen every time you speak. But each time, there will be something good that you can take from the experience and something that you can improve upon.

When you're starting out, write down the good things that happen, as well as the constructive feedback. You're learning and growing, and this will build your confidence over time.

2.3 Authenticity

Professional speaking is about the audience, but it's also about you. When you're 'on' you need to become a 150% version of you, but the energy that you bring to the speaking platform isn't something that can be lived all the time. We all portray different sides of ourselves in a variety of situations. We behave differently with our partners than we do with our parents, children or work colleagues. That's just different sides of you, and they are all genuine and real.

So, your speaking is a performance, but it should also be an authentic one.

You can share your lessons learned, and problems overcome without being perceived as less of an expert or compromising your position. I find that sharing my failures helps me connect far more than pretending that everything has always been fine. Vulnerability as a speaker will enable the audience to see you as a real person, and they will learn far more from you. People connect with people, so be real and human, not super-human!

Tell your own stories

As a speaker, your aim is to connect with people, and the best way is through a story that illustrates the point you want to make. If you're speaking on a topic that you're passionate about, telling stories will be easy, as your own experiences can act as material.

Using props or acting out stories using physical movement can be powerful, as Mark McGuinness explains:

"If I'm talking about Time Management, for instance, I will talk about how disorganized I used to be years ago when I was just struggling. I was on the hamster wheel of email and phone calls coming in, I wasn't getting anything done, and my to-do list was on little curled-up Post-Its that had fallen down behind the desk. It was just a nightmare.

So **I tell that story, and when I'm scrabbling around on the floor for the Post-Its, I look up, and there are people who are going, "That's me."**

Once you've shown them, "Hey, I'm a human being, I had this problem too, and, you know what, I've got a solution," then they will be eager for that. So **you get them involved emotionally by telling a story** that they can relate to."

Mark McGuinness, WishfulThinking.co.uk

Use your own photos

Take photos whenever you can, even when things are difficult. Own your mistakes. I have a picture of me from 2008 proudly standing in front of boxes of my first book, printed in order to sell, make gazillions of dollars and change lives all over the world.

At that moment, I had no idea that 90% of those books would end up in a landfill due to the advent of ebooks and print-on-demand. But that mistake led to me starting my site, TheCreativePenn.com, and then to publishing on the Kindle, then onwards to my speaking career, hundreds of thousands of book sales and eventually leaving my corporate job for a full-time career as an author-entrepreneur.

I'm so glad I have that picture because it represents a hugely expensive error but also the cusp of great change. When I recount the story, I show that picture of a younger me, with hopeful eyes, a proud smile, and no clue of what was about to happen.

Credibility and emotional resonance

The mistakes I've made as an author connect me to the audience and help them far more than prescriptive tips, as well as adding depth to the talk. The feedback later suggests that many of these personal stories are what people remember, and they help to anchor the participants to the more informational material.

It gives more weight to my words when I show how I've failed and moved on into achievement. I know the mistakes of new authors because I have made them myself, and I can demonstrate how to avoid them. I know about changing careers from corporate cubicle slave to creative entrepreneur because I have made that change.

An important part of authenticity is not lying, fabricating, or otherwise trying to make out that you're something you're not. If someone asks you a question and you don't know the answer, just be honest and tell them that you can find out and email them later.

Whatever your life experience, draw on what will resonate with others. Connect with them, and you don't need to be a superstar to make a difference in people's lives.

Always remember to bring the general back to the specific. So, the big message might be "You can change your life," but delivering that in the guise of specific stories is the only effective way to get that across.

What have you done in your life that you can bring to your talk? What personal experiences can you relate that will help people anchor the nebulous to the specific?

What if you're worried about oversharing?

Authenticity is about self-revelation, not exposure, and you have to draw the line where you want to. For example, I don't share my husband's name in public. We have different surnames, so it's not something that is obvious, and in this way, I protect his privacy. Other speakers do the same to protect their children.

However, it's also important to remember that the talk is not about you or your own therapy; it's about the audience. So, be personal but, primarily, share what is useful to them.

Part 3: Practicalities of the speaking business

3.1 How to get speaking work

One of the major things that stop introverts getting speaking engagements is fear of pitching, cold calling and the hard-core sales process that many speakers say you have to do in order to get work. But with the magic of the internet, that is no longer the case, and introverts may actually have the advantage online, as we find it easier to express ourselves alone at a screen.

Here are some of the ways in which you can attract speaking work if you want to make it an income-generating part of your creative business.

(1) Make it clear that you're a speaker

It can be hard to claim the word at first, but if you want to be a speaker, you need to start by saying it out loud and making it clear in your online presence. Add a speaking page to your website and include the word 'Speaker' on your business card. When you meet people, say that you're a speaker, and add it to your email signature.

(2) Attract attention online

Blogging and creating audio or video, as well as connecting on social media can attract opportunities instead of you having to seek them out. This is certainly not a short cut, as it takes a lot of work to build this kind of presence online, but it's a great way to do it if you're not keen on pitching. There's more on content marketing later in this section.

95% of my speaking work has happened because of my blog and social media presence, and adventurer Alastair Humphreys credits it for his success too.

> "I made the decision to blog properly and to really start blogging a lot and to spread my word through the blog ecosystem and all the aspects of online marketing. That made the biggest difference of all, I think, for both my fees and my number of talks."

(3) Volunteer for free speaking events

When you first get started, it's a good idea to speak for free. This will build your confidence and, if you do a good job, it might lead to other opportunities. You never know who might be in the audience that day, who they know or how they are connected. You just have to put yourself out there.

(4) Go to networking events

Introverts are more comfortable with one-on-one conversations, so networking events can be intimidating, especially when you walk into a room of noisy people. Although you may need to psych yourself up for it (as I do), networking events are a fantastic way to meet new people, and there will likely be other introverts in the room feeling the way you are too. Start a conversation on the edges of the main gathering, and you'll soon get into the swing of it.

Ensure that you network in your target market. For example, I speak to those people running small businesses and individuals who want to become creative entrepreneurs, so there's no point in me networking with employees who are happy working in large corporates because that's not currently my target market.

You can find many networking events locally or on MeetUp. com, but you can also find groups online using twitter hashtags or discussion groups on Facebook or LinkedIn.

(5) Pitch for speaking events

Many conferences and events will open for pitches six months before the event, so you can submit your proposal for a talk if you keep an eye out for opportunities. These are often online forms, so there's no pitching in person, a relief for introverts! You'll need an appropriate and catchy topic as well as a good speaking page with testimonials so that the conference organizers can find out more about you. This method is how I got the opportunity to speak at the London Book Fair a few years ago.

It can be useful to attend a conference first before pitching to speak, so you understand the audience expectations and the vibe.

(6) Speaking bureaux

More established speakers may want to join a bureau or agency or work with an agent. They work on commission, so you'll need to be making a significant amount per talk in order to make it worthwhile, but they can often get you work if you have an appropriate topic.

Of course, you can also pitch in person and network with conference organizers, but the options above are probably best for introverts!

3.2 Running your own public events

It's easier than ever to organize your own events with online tools these days. It's a great way to increase your revenue, as you get a greater percentage of income by running the event yourself. Here are some points to take into consideration.

Ticketing

Eventbrite.com is the most well-known ticketing service, and it also has built-in marketing, as people are notified of events in their area. You can set up deadlines, early bird pricing, discount codes, number limits, and everything you need for an event, including sales tax details. There's a Facebook app for direct booking and social amplification, and people can pay by credit card or PayPal as well as using mobile check-in.

Eventbee is a competitor to Eventbrite and offers all of the same functionality as well as specific seating numbering, which may be appropriate in a small number of cases. It also works out cheaper if you're using the PayPal option, and both sites charge a per ticket fee.

If you have your own website and already sell products, you can use your own online store or even just a PayPal button. I have used e-Junkie, SELZ, and Payhip to create my own PDF tickets with just a button on my site.

As an introvert, I hate calling on the phone to book something, so I will generally not book if it has to be done with a phone call. Always have an online option if you're running your own events.

Venue

If you live in a large city, then you can often sort the venue out after the initial ticket sales, as there are so many options for meeting spaces. This means that you can use some of the ticket money for the venue deposit. But if you're just starting out, you will need to do some venue scouting first.

Here are some questions to consider when choosing a venue:

- Is it close to transport hubs and/or parking?

- Is it close to amenities for food or coffee for breaks and lunch? (or you need to ensure that there's adequate catering included)

- Does the room have enough space for your audience without being cramped?

- Is there a break-out space for eating, coffee or breaks and somewhere for smokers or vaping?

- Does it have natural light and adequate airflow, especially for full-day events? You'll also need the capacity for shade or blackout if you're using slides or showing videos.

- Does it have proper temperature control, heating, or aircon, depending on your location?

- Does it have the required technology, for example, screen and projector? Do you need a tech person to help set up?

- Does it have appropriate accessibility for those who need it?

One of the worst venues I have worked in was a box room with no natural light and no temperature control for a full day. The energy drain was tremendous, and maintaining attention in the afternoon was practically impossible. When you visit a venue, try to imagine it full of people and then make decisions based on that. You can also note down appropriate venues as you attend events over time.

Organizing a venue for a multi-day retreat is a lot more complicated, especially when it's international. This is something I want to move into at some point, but most likely with a logistics partner locally.

Sales Page

If you use one of the online ticketing tools, you build a sales page onto the ticketing site itself, but it's also a good idea to have a specific sales page on your own website with buttons that link through to the ticketing site. Your sales page should include:

- Title of the event: catchy, appropriate, and search engine friendly. What do your customers want?

- Description of the event, focusing on the benefits to the customer and what they will learn

- Cost, with early bird pricing if possible

- Biographies for you and other speakers

- Venue details, or general physical location if setting up the sales page early

- Start and end times

- Call to action, for example, "Book now to reserve your place." You might think that a call to action is unnecessary, but studies have shown that you get a higher response rate if you specifically ask for action.

You can find an example of a sales page in Appendix 4.

Marketing and advertising

The ticketing sites mentioned have a built-in search function, so people looking for specific events may find yours. Make sure to use keywords that people search for in the title and description, so that your event shows up in search results.

If you have built your own email list, covered later in this section, then start by emailing everyone on it. If your list is local to your area, you will likely start the booking process that way. You can also put an announcement on your website, perhaps a banner or button pointing to the registration form, and if you have a podcast, announce it there, too.

Use social media to draw attention to the event, making sure to focus on the benefit to the customer and what they will get out of it.

If you have an established platform, it's likely that you will be able to sell out the tickets using these methods. You can also use geographically-targeted advertising like paid Facebook or Instagram ads to reach more people.

Practicalities of the event

Running your own events often means you have to do your own technical setup, and sometimes even provide your own screen and projector for slides if you're using them. You can often hire this equipment cheaply, but make sure that you allow enough time to set it all up and sort out any technical issues.

You'll also need to meet and greet, check people off the

attendee list and answer any practical questions, so it's a good idea to get someone else to help you, at least at the start.

Catering is a key decision. Even something basic will increase your costs, but if you're charging a higher ticket price, then you need to include food. Coffee or tea, as well as soft drinks and water, should always be included. If you're not feeding people, you need to make sure that there are local food outlets so that people don't leave and travel too far from the venue. If you are catering, include a section for dietary requirements on the booking form.

Pros and cons of running your own event

If you're just the speaker, everything is organized for you in terms of venue, attendees, equipment, tech setup, and if there's travel, that's often sorted out as well. You don't have to meet and greet; you just have to be there on time, speak well, chat to attendees, and then leave. No fuss, no setup, no cleanup. Fantastic!

However, you can often earn more money if you organize events yourself. Here's a worked example.

Let's say you do a full-day seminar for $150 per head and have 30 people attending, for a total of $4500

Take out the venue fee $1000, catering $600, equipment hire $200, booking fees $450. Total costs: $2250

You're still left with $2250

For this type of event, just as the speaker, you should be able to negotiate at least $800 - $1000 but you'll always have to share the revenue with the person running it. That's just some approximate math, and of course, there is a huge amount of variability from industry to industry.

If you do run an event yourself, start small and minimize risk

Don't start by organizing a multi-speaker conference in a hotel with full catering and a huge deposit. Start with a small venue and a small seminar to build your confidence and learn from each event.

To sum up, it's higher risk, more work ,and a potentially greater reward to organize events yourself. It's less stressful but with potentially lower returns to be the speaker at an established event. Perhaps the best balance is to do a bit of both.

3.3 Marketing your speaking business

In the next few chapters, I'll go through the essentials for marketing your speaking as well as some of the extra ways that you can attract speaking work if you want to make it a core part of your creative business.

I go into more detail in *How to Market a Book,* and much of marketing remains the same, whether you're attracting people to your book, your speaker services or any other kind of small business. I have reframed the following chapters towards speakers instead of authors.

3.4 Generosity, social karma, and co-opetition

We speak because we want to help people by providing information or inspiration, or we want to entertain people and make them think. Consider marketing in the same way and focus on the customer, not on you. This serves several purposes:

- It makes you think about what they really want

- It takes the focus off you and stops you feeling self-conscious

- It gives you ideas as to what to share in your marketing

- It helps you connect with a community of other speakers

Generosity and social karma

The word karma implies that you get back what you give, and I believe that this is true in the online marketing environment.

> Being useful, helpful, and generous is satisfying to you personally, but also builds up a bank of goodwill that will come back to you in a different way.

This can be applicable to your audience at a speaking engagement or online, as well as to your community of other speakers. I've found my fellow travelers on the journey to be important in my development as an author, speaker, and entrepreneur. Their friendship, support, advice, and sharing of business opportunities have been vital for my own personal growth as well as my income.

If you focus on generosity first, people are attracted to you in an authentic manner. When you later mention that you are looking for speaking engagements or have a book out, people are more likely to help you or buy.

This approach is based on the science of influence. Read Robert Cialdini's book, *Influence: The Psychology of Persuasion*, and you'll understand that the principle of reciprocity is one of the keys to influencing people's behavior, but it's important to do it in an ethical way.

Co-opetition

Co-opetition is about cooperating with your perceived competition so that both parties benefit. When there is a congruence of interest, cooperating together can create greater value than acting alone.

Join a network of speakers locally or even internationally and share your lessons learned, pass on opportunities, and refer other speakers. In working together, we can learn lessons faster, respond to the market, and adapt more quickly.

Once you start to become successful, there will never be enough hours in the day to do all of the speaking opportunities that will come your way. You can please clients as well as speaker associates by referring specialists in the same area as you, and they will end up doing the same.

You can also do the same with marketing. For example, interview each other on your respective blogs, share news of a book release or workshop launch, attend each other's talks, and help with feedback or video.

If you do this consistently, without expecting a return, you will find favors repaid, sometimes from other sources and in surprising ways.

The importance of know, like and trust

Marketing from a personal perspective is about people getting to know, like, and trust us, and everything that I do online is focused on being authentic.

For example, I include photos on my Twitter and Instagram timelines that only tangentially relate to a speaking event. For example, after speaking at a seminar in Berlin, I posted a picture of the ancient Babylonian Ishtar Gate, which appears in my thriller, *End of Days*. Pictures like that enable people to get to know me a little more and have a glimpse into my world. I'm not trying to sell anything, just share a bit about my interests and, hopefully, attract like minds.

Of course, almost everything I do is somehow related to my speaking, books, or to my creative business. But I don't share pictures of my husband or my family, as that is personal and also not relevant, and I've drawn a line for privacy. You will need to find your own balance.

3.5 Your speaker brand

"When you build your brand, opportunities come to you."

Mark McGuinness, WishfulThinking.co.uk

Deciding on your niche is one thing, but deciding on your brand takes it further, as it provides nuance and depth to a general topic, for example, two speakers might talk about creative productivity in two very different ways.

You have a brand, whether you like it or not

It's how people perceive you.

Having a brand doesn't mean that you need an expensive logo or unique design (although you can do these things). It's the emotions, words, and images that you and your name evoke.

When someone meets you in person, they make a judgment about you based on how you look, how you interact, how you perform, and what you're passionate about. When someone finds your website or social media profile online, they make the same kind of judgment. They will decide whether they're interested in you very quickly.

Your job is to make your message clear through your branding. You want to attract your target audience and turn off those who aren't your type of people. You need to actively shape your brand, so you are in control of those perceptions.

Deciding on your brand

Consider the following questions:

What specific topic do you speak on? What **words** do you want people to associate with you?

What is the tone of your speaking? Are you inspirational or motivational? Are you a teacher? Do you have gravitas and authority? Are you funny and playful?

What **images** do you want to be associated with you and your brand? What colors resonate for you and communicate your tone?

What are your **goals** for the next few years? What words are associated with those?

Who do you admire and want to emulate as a speaker and as a brand? Find their websites and keep screen-prints of what you like and don't like. Use them as a **model** (but obviously no plagiarism!)

You also need to know **what you want for your future**, because if you can't see this brand extending over many years, you have hard work ahead! I made this mistake at the beginning of my speaking career when I branded myself with 'career change' and a business-focused, pin-stripe suit image. I quickly realized that I didn't want to speak or write on that topic anymore and started The Creative Penn, a new brand, around writing and creativity. This developed into a platform for my non-fiction books as well as professional speaking, and it allows me to speak and write around anything to do with creativity.

Examples of speaker brands

Here are some great speaker brand examples. I've heard these speakers live, and they definitely speak like the brand they present online.

Dr. Janet Lapp

I heard Janet speak at a convention several years ago, and she has remained with me as an example to emulate through her professionalism and her authenticity in sharing personal stories.

Janet's site at Lapp.com is simple, inviting, and professional. The word 'Change' is dominant, indicating her niche. There's a video of her speaking and also an image of her book with testimonials as social proof. A book is a great way to encapsulate your brand and can become a key part of your speaking engagements.

Janet also uses professional credentials, displaying the logo of the NSA, the National Speakers Association in the USA. CSP stands for Certified Speaking Professional and indicates that she has attained a specific level of excellence. Her About page includes information on her professional background as a nurse, her Ph.D. in Psychology, and the fact she is a Flight Instructor, which adds a certain fearlessness to her brand.

There is a blog for content marketing and a list of keynotes she can give, as well as a button to Request a Keynote.

Alastair Humphreys: adventurer, author, and motivational speaker

AlastairHumphreys.com is dominated by images of Alastair's adventures and travels in exotic places: walking through the desert, across frozen ice, rowing the Atlantic and cycling around the world. There is a clear link to a speaking page which has a picture of him speaking at TEDx in a smarter outfit. His message is clearly visible on the screen behind, "Why not start today?"

There are testimonials from the UK Special Forces, Google, Facebook, the Royal Geographical Society, and England Rugby. Alastair's social proof is also evident in being named National Geographic's Adventurer of the Year. Alastair's brand is very clear from his site, his images, and the words he uses in the chosen text and testimonials.

He also has a regular blog, an email newsletter, and a very active social media presence where he shares photos from his many travels which bring people to his site.

Jeremy Nicholas

The tagline at JeremyNicholas.co.uk is "Keeping conference delegates awake since 1994," which immediately communicates that he is a funny guy with a lot of experience.

The images and video on his home page feature laughing and smiling delegates at corporate events, clearly indicating his target market and his services.

Humor pervades the site which also conveys professionalism in terms of the testimonials. If it makes you smile, you might consider booking Jeremy as a speaker. Having seen Jeremy in action, the site resonates with how he speaks. It will turn some people off but absolutely attract the kind of person he is aiming at.

Susan Cain

Susan speaks about introversion relating to her books on the same topic, including *Quiet: The Power of Introverts in a World That Can't Stop Talking*.

Her main site is QuietRev.com which has a page dedicated to her speaking with pictures of her at events, the topics she speaks on, and a form for speaking requests which includes the option for virtual attendance. She has also blogged about her struggles around learning to speak and ultimately, how she tackled those fears in order to share her important message more widely than in books. It has certainly worked, and her TED talk has been watched over 23 million times.

She is also represented by a number of speaker bureaux including Speaking.com which have more sales-focused information including her rates which fall in the range of $30,000 - $50,000. Don't let anyone tell you that introverted speakers can't make a good living!

A creative who speaks, but doesn't really want to

Neil Gaiman is a bestselling and award-winning dark fantasy author and screenwriter, one of the few fiction authors who speak professionally. However, he rarely speaks because he is so busy creating books and TV series like American Gods, Coraline, and Good Omens.

On his website, NeilGaiman.com, he has an Appearance page which gives directions for how to approach his agent and notes:

"Tell him you want me to appear somewhere. Have him tell you how much it costs. Have him say it again in case you misheard it the first time … it's true, I'm not cheap. On the other hand, I'm really busy, and I ought to be writing, so pricing appearances somewhere between ridiculously high and obscenely high helps to discourage most of the people who want me to come and talk to them. Which I could make a full-time profession, if I didn't say no a lot."

I have another brand and writing existence as J.F.Penn, thriller writer, so I like Neil's attitude. Of course, he has hit the big time with his books, and most authors need to do many other things to make a living, but this might be something to aspire to!

Focus on you

With all these examples of speaker branding, the focus is on the speaker and what makes them special. It can be hard to write information that seems self-promotional, but if you want to be a paid professional speaker, you need to frame your online brand so that people know what you represent and whether you fit with what they want, and understand what they will get if they book you. They should not be surprised by your performance as it will resonate with your online brand.

You can absolutely change your brand over time, but you do need to start with some idea of how you want to be perceived.

3.6 Website and speaker's page

Ideally, you need a website that you can update and maintain yourself, and it should include a great speaker's page that helps to sell your services. You can use your site to attract opportunity, which I'll explain later in chapter 3.9 on content marketing.

One of the biggest mistakes I see is paying a company or freelancer way too much for a website. You don't need to do that! It's cheap and easy to set up a website yourself these days.

> Here's my video tutorial on how to set up your own website in around 30 minutes using WordPress: TheCreativePenn.com/authorwebsite

The tutorial is aimed at authors, but the principles still apply for speakers.

The second mistake is not learning how to maintain your site yourself.

It takes a day or so of concentrated effort to learn WordPress, and you'll save yourself a lot of money and heartache if you can adjust your own site over time. If you're sharing content and actively working in your niche, you'll end up adjusting your site weekly, even daily.

It's important to get started with a site even when you don't have much of a clue technically, because it's easier to change direction once you're moving, and it's easier to update something that already has a framework. This is similar to writing a book, where you can only edit something that exists as a first draft. So get the first draft of your website sorted, and then update it over time as you grow and learn.

Don't obsess over design

The beauty of using software like WordPress is that you can get fantastic free designs or pay a little extra for premium themes that make your site highly customizable. You can easily change the theme at any point without impacting your content. They are also mobile-optimized, so your site looks good on any device.

Build your site with a clean, easy-to-read, simple design, and update later. I've been through several redesigns in the last ten years of TheCreativePenn.com, and no doubt I will continue to change things over time.

Get to know your new home on the internet

Once your site is available, get in there and play. You don't need to be a programmer to use a WordPress site. It's mainly drag and drop and clicking buttons, like MS Word on steroids.

Add some content and, over time, learn how the features of WordPress work. Discover plugins and widgets and cool stuff that you can do with your site. But at least learn how to update a page and a post, how to add an image and how to link to other sites and your own sales pages. It's worth a few hours of learning and will save you a lot of time and money in the future.

Your speaker page

If you want to be a professional speaker, one of the first things I recommend is setting up a speaker page. Here are the main elements to include:

- Information about you, including a bio that may be used as an introduction

- A list of topics that you speak on with a brief description or even specific landing pages per topic

- Testimonials from previous attendees or event organizers

- Photos of you in action, or at least a professional headshot as well as video clips if possible. You can add these over time as you get some bigger speaking events under your belt.

- How to contact you for booking inquiries

- Your availability, with upcoming and previous engagements if applicable

- Press kit or clippings, used as social proof and evidence of your reach

It's not recommended to include any kind of fee schedule, as you will likely adapt your speaker fee to the occasion.

As an example, you can find my speaker page at TheCreativePenn.com/speaking and you can also model your own page on speakers you find compelling in your niche.

Don't worry about making it perfect. Just put something basic up when you get started and add to it over time. By creating that page, you will be claiming your future and announcing to the world that you are available.

Create a business card with the word 'Speaker' on it and link to your speaking page. You're now officially available!

3.7 Professional photos

Professional speakers need a number of different photos, but the headshot is critical for all of your marketing material, so focus on that first. Action shots will come over time from the various events you speak at, but your face is unique, and people connect with people, so you need a good photo on your site. An event organizer may come to your website because of your reputation or through search, but how you present yourself from this very first moment is critical, so don't use an amateur shot.

Here are some tips for your professional photos.

Preparation

Decide on what kind of photos you need and how they will communicate your brand. I have two brands, JF Penn, thriller author, and Joanna Penn, professional speaker and non-fiction author, but both are me. I decided to have my professional photos done in Oxford, where I went to university, as well as where some of my fiction is set. It also has some incredible architecture that make the photos more interesting, especially in black and white with a serious expression evoking thriller, or in smiling color for my speaker page.

Research appropriate photographers

Many things these days can be done online, but physical pictures of you need to be done in person so Google "portrait photographer" plus the place you live or want to have photos in. I looked specifically for Oxford photographers. Then go through their sites to get an idea of the type of pictures they take as well as their prices for your budget. You want to feel happy with how they do things and the results they get.

After some research, I went with Mim Saxl, whose portrait shots set in Oxford are casual, yet professional, and I also liked her attitude and pricing. Email or phone the photographer to set up times and dates as well as any other details. Discuss your thoughts on branding and type of shot. Communication is critical and if you struggle with talking about what you want, make sure that you write it down, so the photographer is aware of your thoughts, or find pictures of other speakers whose images you like.

Try on different outfits

My photographer, Mim, told me that plain colors work best for headshots as they don't draw attention away from the face. I was having photos taken outside in May, which should have been warm, but I'm in England, so, of course, it was absolutely freezing. Definitely bring different clothing options for changing weather conditions. Even if you're inside, take a few changes of clothes so that you can do different looking shots.

The photoshoot

Look your best. If you're paying for pro photos then paying for some professional makeup and hair may also be a good idea if you're not confident doing it yourself, but be sure to still look like you! In general, make sure the look matches your brand, for example, for men, stubble may be just right for the casual brand, or you might need to shave and wear a suit.

Trust the photographer

You've hired a professional for a reason. They will take a lot of shots, and many of them will be terrible. That's OK. They know what they're doing. Trust them and let them guide you in terms of location and positioning.

Imagine someone you love behind the lens for a more personal look and depth to your smile

You see some pictures of authors, in particular, looking scared or just unhappy in their head-shots. Try to be natural and move through different expressions as the photographer clicks away. Keep imagining a real person smiling at you if you're smiling at the camera. Anyone can tell a fake smile by looking at your eyes, so make sure that they are real smiles.

Have fun!

A good photographer will help you relax and come up with some great shots. Sit back, and enjoy the ride.

3.8 Email marketing

Your email list is a critical part of your business because it enables you to reach people over time.

You have control over your message, and you don't have to rely on other people or companies to bring you income. If you have something useful to say or share that relates to your niche, email your list. If you're doing a workshop, email your list. If you have a book out that supports your speaking topic, email your list.

Through email, you can build up a relationship with people over the long term, so that they get to know who you are. Despite the proliferation of social media, email is still a great way to communicate, and it's much more direct, targeted, and relational than the social platforms.

Permission marketing

There are plenty of people who use email lists badly and in a way that makes many people uncomfortable. You don't have to do that because there is a way to use lists and email marketing with integrity.

The phrase 'permission marketing' was coined by marketing guru Seth Godin in his book of the same name. It *"is the privilege (not the right) of delivering anticipated, personal and relevant messages to people who actually want to get them."*

Permission is even more important in an age of GDPR, which means that companies can be fined if they breach data privacy or protection guidelines.

For a free webinar on how to be GDPR compliant, check out: TheCreativePenn.com/gdprhelp

But don't let the guidelines put you off. It's just about being ethical around building an email list and how you communicate with people once they sign up. Permission marketing works as follows:

People choose to give you their email address

Either in exchange for something specific, for example, a free ebook like my Author 2.0 Blueprint, or because they want updates from you or want to know when your next speaking event is. They need to actively sign up or agree to be on your list. When I'm speaking, I tell people that they can get the Author 2.0 Blueprint if they go sign up at my website. This ensures that only the people who are specifically interested make the effort. The number of people on your list is less important than how engaged they are.

You can put a physical paper sign up sheet in the room or pass it around but make sure it includes clear information about what people are signing up for so they give informed consent to be emailed. You'll also need to make sure you include a link to your Privacy Policy which details how you collect and store data.

Respect your list

Keep their details private and don't sell your list or buy list members from other sources.

Never sign people up to your list if you just think they will be interested. I get spam emails every day from people who have signed me up for their lists, which I delete immediately. I use a specific private email address for lists that I personally sign up to, so I always know when someone has signed me up manually without my permission.

The email system that I use, ConvertKit, has double-opt-in which means that when a person is added to the list, they have to confirm that they want to be on it, even after they have signed up. This is an anti-spam mechanism that helps to ensure permission. I also have a personal rule that I will never add people to my list manually. People have to sign up themselves, so I know that everyone on my list should really be there.

You have permission to email but only with information relating to what they signed up for

For example, I couldn't start emailing my Creative Penn list with information on weight loss products. I only email about topics relating to writing, publishing, book marketing, and creative entrepreneurship because that's what people have signed up for.

For my JFPenn list, I only email about my fiction, or about other thrillers, research and other things that particular audience is interested in. I also have BooksAndTravel. page where I share a monthly reading list. You may need to maintain separate lists if you have more than one niche, as I do.

Make sure it's easy for people to unsubscribe. There is a way to unsubscribe with one click at the bottom of all good email services that comply with anti-spam laws. You *want* people to unsubscribe if they're unhappy with what they are getting from you. Remember that your speaking topic, books, and products are not for everyone!

So, how do you build a list?

(1) Sign up for a list management service

There are lots of options, but I recommend ConvertKit, which I use personally and is one of the best and most highly reputable services.

It is very simple to set up forms and paste them into your site, so there's no programming needed, and there is a lot of help information. It has a scalable monthly fee depending on how many names you store. If you sign up for my Author 2.0 Blueprint, you will see how the service works from a user point of view.

There are many other options, so check the terms of service and Google the latest comparisons between them to see what suits you the best.

(2) Set up a form

A webform is a place where the customer can enter their name, email, and anything else you want to capture.

You can see an example on the Author 2.0 Blueprint sign-up page at:

TheCreativePenn.com/blueprint

(3) Set up the emails

You need to set up a welcome email that people get straight away, and you can also set up Sequences, a series of automatic emails that are sent at specific intervals.

My Author 2.0 Blueprint list has a series of emails that come every week with aspects of writing, publishing, book marketing, and making a living with your writing.

This type of email sequence is great for non-fiction authors and speakers in particular, as you can give people more useful information about your niche expertise, and if they continue to read your emails, then they will get to know, like and trust you over time.

You can use the Broadcast mechanism to send sporadic email newsletters or notification of sales, events, or book launches.

Test the form signup and emails by signing up yourself and sending yourself a newsletter, just to make sure that everything is OK, and then you're ready to go!

(4) Make sure that the list can be found on your site

It's great to have your list signup form 'above the fold,' which is somewhere it can be seen without scrolling. You can also have a bigger page that you link to elsewhere. Make sure that it works on mobile as this is increasingly the most common form of browsing.

After you have set up the mechanism for sign-up, you can drive people to the list using the usual traffic building activities like blogging, social media and other activities, including telling people about it when you speak.

> Remember, you want to be a valuable resource to people, either for information, inspiration, or entertainment.

You do not ever want to be seen as a spammer. So give away great information on a regular basis for free, and people will be happy to buy from you when you have something they're interested in. Don't send unrelated offers. Don't abuse the list, or they will unsubscribe. It's all about respect.

Email marketing over time

Once you've started your list, don't wait too long before sending out an update. This will differ depending on what you promised at signup and also what else you're doing with your website. Your updates could include:

- **News and articles** about your industry or niche. This will usually involve links to other resources.

- **Your own articles, audio or video.** This might include personal items like photos or anything else to make it personal.

- **News** about your speaking engagements and book or product releases

- **Competitions,** giveaways and anything relevant to your audience that will benefit them

You want people to open your emails, so make them interesting and **include a headline** that will make them want to read on.

You also need to send emails regularly enough so it is not a surprise when you do send one. Don't just email when you have something to sell. Build a relationship over time. Fans want to know what you're up to, and they will be interested in what you have to share with them. I also try to make things more personal by sharing photos of what I've been up to lately.

There are no rules! The bare minimum is to have a simple list of people to notify when you have a speaking engagement coming up, or a book or product coming out, so get started on building your email list today.

If you need more help, check out my tutorial on how to set up your mailing list with ConvertKit:

TheCreativePenn.com/setup-email-list

3.9 Content marketing

"I made the decision to blog properly and to
really start blogging a lot … and use all aspects of
online marketing. That made the biggest difference of all
for both my fees and my number of talks."

Alastair Humphreys, adventurer

Content marketing is creating free material like articles, video, or audio in order to attract people who might go on to buy your books, products, or speaking services.

This type of marketing suits introverts in particular, as it doesn't involve large groups of people, cold calling, or any form of hard-core sales. It can be done in private and on your own time.

Content marketing is the engine that drives my business. I've been blogging and podcasting for over ten years, and it brings hundreds of thousands of people to my website every month driving sales as well as attracting speaking opportunities. It's also global, with people in 218 countries accessing my content online. Exciting times, indeed!

Content marketing ISN'T: a personal blog for sharing holiday photos or tweets about your breakfast, or YouTube videos unrelated to your niche.

Content marketing IS: articles, audio, video, or images in a specific niche that are designed to attract your target market who might go on to purchase your speaking, books, products, or services.

Content marketing can help you stand out in a crowded market

The internet is full of free information, entertainment, and inspiration. That's what people generally go looking for when they search online. There are millions of sites that will give them what they want, and it's easy to get lost in the myriad options.

In order to stand out, you need to have an online presence with quality content specific to your target audience. It should also resonate with your personality and authentic brand. I've found that the more personal the content, the more engaged the audience will be.

Each piece of content you put out there is another way for someone to discover you.

If people find you and want to stay on your site, if they are happy to give you their email address, this means you have permission to talk to them, and eventually they might book you to speak or buy your book, product or service.

That is the goal of content marketing.

You provide good quality, useful, entertaining, or inspirational content that brings people to your site. They begin to know you, like you and trust you, and when you have something to sell — a speaking engagement, a book or product — they might consider buying it.

Content marketing is great for introverts

Introverts are often more comfortable with sharing personally when removed from face-to-face interaction. You don't need to engage in small talk, you can get straight to what really matters, so we can touch people from afar using these methods of content marketing.

You can set it all up from the comfort of your own desk, in the quiet of your own home. You can interact with comments or social media responses when you're in the mood to socialize.

There's no hard sell, no cold calling, no need for pushiness. It's authentic attraction marketing

What types of content can you produce?

Here are just a few examples, but there really is no limit these days.

Text articles related to your niche

Write high-quality articles for your own website that give great value. You can also write guest posts on other blogs within your niche and aim to get on bigger blogs with a wider audience. Learn about search engine optimization and make sure you use a catchy, well-targeted headline.

Video

Google owns YouTube, and video makes up a growing percentage of search, especially in specific niches and demographics. Mobile video is also on the rise as streaming bandwidth improves, and many social media sites now favor video.

You can do interviews, talking head opinion pieces, funny skits, vlog chat shows, book trailers, on-location research videos, and many more options. More on video in chapter 3.11.

Audio

Podcasting has exploded in the last few years because of the ease of downloading and listening on mobile devices. I've been podcasting for over ten years with The Creative Penn Podcast, and it remains my favorite form of content marketing. I also have the Books and Travel Podcast for people who, you guessed it, like books and travel.

When people listen to your voice for 30 minutes or more per week, when they hear you laugh and talk about aspects of your life, they feel like they know you. Building trust and rapport is key to content marketing, and both audio and video are brilliant ways to do this. More on audio in chapter 3.12.

White paper, ebook or free report

My Author 2.0 Blueprint is an example of this. It contains ideas that you can use to write, publish, sell and promote your book on the internet right away, for free, and people sign up for it every day because it provides useful information. It's the way I build my email list, so it's valuable content marketing.

Webinar

You can do live events easily now using paid services like GoToWebinar as well as many free options. When people listen to your expertise, ask questions, and engage with you, it can result in immediate opportunities because you have a personal connection.

Webinars can be used to generate leads and sales of audio and video courses as well as services. There are many online conferences with multiple speakers, which can be a fantastic way to get speaking practice, so watch out for those opportunities. Just make sure it's the right target audience for you as well as a brand you want to be associated with.

Photos or images that relate to your niche or your speaking life

You can also share images on sites like Instagram and Pinterest that draw people into your eco-system. You can see some of my pictures on Instagram @jfpennauthor.

These can be a way to get initial attention but make sure that your bio has a link to something they may want to sign up for so you can continue the relationship beyond the image.

Re-purpose your content for maximum reach

You can write a text article then record it as a video and/or a podcast, include it in your email newsletter or create a slideshow from it as well as sharing it on social media sites. There are no limits to content marketing options, and new tools emerge all the time. If you find it too overwhelming, or beyond your time constraints, you can hire virtual assistants or companies that specialize in re-purposing content.

Content marketing vs. social media

Some people confuse these terms, so here's the difference:

With content marketing, you actually **create something new and original in the world.** It could be a blog post, a video, a podcast, an infographic or image, or an ebook giveaway.

You own it and host it somewhere that you can control. The content draws people into finding out more about you, your speaking services, books, and products. An exception to this might be strategic guest posting or interviews on someone else's show where you talk to a different audience.

The content lasts a long time and continues to be relevant. It can be found in search engines, and people may consume it or link back to it years later. For example, people who discover my podcast on episode 400 might go back and listen to several years of backlist interviews. This is a good reason to focus on evergreen content, rather than news items that lose their relevance over time.

Social media is immediate and **ephemeral**, designed to catch attention at the point when someone is there in the moment. Posts on Twitter, Facebook, Instagram, and other social media appear briefly on timelines and then sink quickly as other content emerges.

You don't own the platform, so it can disappear at any point

You should never build your entire platform on someone else's site because when the rules change, your business is impacted. It may even disappear. Some people put everything into mySpace years ago, and then it sank with the rise of Facebook and Instagram, but the rules continue to change, and organic reach has become pay to play. Definitely use the tools, but build the base of your platform on your own hosted site and use social media amplification.

Always drive people back to your site. Link to your own content, share other people's content, and join in discussions to foster interactive relationships.

It is critical to build quality, long-lasting, original content if you want to become known online. The rules are the same whether you're a speaker, an author, or anyone else who wants to make a living online.

The internet compounds over time. It takes time to grow.

We all start with nothing. No traffic to our site. No sales. No social media followers. No email list.

I started TheCreativePenn.com in 2008, and I spent the first year feeling like I was howling into the wind. But I kept creating — blogging, podcasting, and networking on social media. In 2011, I left my job to become a full-time author-entrepreneur, and now, my multi-six-figure business continues to be powered by my blog and podcast. Speaking opportunities come to me because of my platform. Content marketing does take time, but it's been well worth it for me.

3.10 Social media

Social media is still about hand-selling to individuals, but this time on a global scale. It's about connection and relationships — all human activities.

Remember that behind the profile is a real person. Social media is not about traffic or selling. It's about connecting with people, and the best way to use any of the sites is to be authentic and real. Don't broadcast spammy sales messages, just be yourself.

Do you need social media as part of your marketing?

Nothing is mandatory, and you can definitely have a speaker business without social media, but it is a great way to connect with a group of like-minded people as well as your target market, especially if you're attending events which often have a social media element.

It doesn't take much time if you're disciplined and use scheduling tools like BufferApp, and it makes you and your work shareable.

Twitter has played the most significant role in my own speaker business, because of the relationships and opportunities that have arisen from connections I've made there over the years. You might find other sites work well for your business.

How does social media sell you and your business?

The old adage goes: *"50% of marketing works. We just don't know which 50%."* It is indeed an inexact science, but here's how the marketing principle AIDA works. There are new tools all the time, but the principles are the same regardless.

(1) Attention

Attention is hard to get in this speedy online world. Social media is one way to grab attention for a moment in order to draw people into your marketing funnel. Be interesting, entertaining, or inspirational and be sure to use an enticing headline so that people want to share and hopefully, click on your bio to learn more.

(2) Interest

Social media is pointless on its own as a marketing mechanism (although of course, it can be enjoyed for its own sake). The aim is to get people to notice you and be interested enough to follow you or click through to your website or speaker's page. Make sure that you have your social media links on every page of your site so that you're easy to connect with.

Social media sites rise and fall. You don't own that real estate; you only borrow it for a while, so be sure to capture interest through your website and email list, as described in chapter 3.8.

(3) Desire

It's unlikely that someone would book you for a speaking event based on one contact, as it generally takes time for people to make a buying decision. It can happen, but social media is more of a long-term relationship and word-of-mouth strategy.

Once people have found you and are interested in what you're doing, they might follow your blog, maybe listen to an interview with you or watch a video, and continue to follow you on social media. They might also sign up for your email list.

It's all about inviting people into your eco-system so they can get to know you, like you and trust you enough to give you a slice of their time and attention. Authenticity over the long term is therefore important so you can sustain it and in this way, you foster a desire in your audience to support you or buy from you or book you for a speaking event.

(4) Action

Once people know you, like you and trust you, they are far more likely to come along to one of your events, recommend you as a speaker or buy your books and products. There is no hard sell necessary. Your audience will be ready to take action and buy when you announce an event.

It's about the audience

If you want to get social media right, your focus should be on being useful, inspiring, or entertaining, promoting others, and becoming a trusted voice in your niche. Be personal and of course, promote your own products and events when appropriate but balance that out with other content, so it's not all about you.

Social means social

Social media doesn't work if you don't enjoy it or if you are unrelentingly negative. Networks are collective energy expressed in one place. If you exude negativity or hype or spam, then that's what you will experience in return. It's about enjoying yourself, joining a conversation, learning from people, sharing something interesting, and making connections. Yes, it can be fun!

Some people think that online relationships are somehow shallow or unreal, but for introverts, the online social world is often far preferable to live networking events or parties. Friendships formed on social media can spill into Skype conversations, meeting up in person and support networks, as well as mutual promotion. I've made some of my best 'real-life' friendships on Twitter and done a lot of business through contacts made there.

Of course, social media is not a magic bullet for sales

It's just one tool in the arsenal of marketing activities that some people enjoy. But from my personal, introverted experience, it can definitely result in sales, and it's a lot of fun!

3.11 Video

Video can be daunting, especially for introverts, but it's also incredibly valuable as a speaker. There's a learning curve, like anything else, but I've found it well worth investing in.

There are a number of ways in which video is useful for a speaking business.

(1) A self-improvement tool

It's difficult to be objective when evaluating your own speaking performance. It's also practically impossible to be self-aware about your speaking at the same time as effectively giving your all to an audience.

If you video yourself or have someone else do it, it is much easier to assess your performance objectively later. You may be surprised by what you see and hear, but go easy on yourself, as we can be our own harshest critics.

(2) Evidence of your speaking ability

When an organization is considering booking you for a speaking event, they will look for evidence that you can deliver on your promise. Once you're established, you'll get a lot of repeat business from the same places, or recommendations from testimonials, but at the beginning, it's hard to get this evidence.

I started out using a small video camera in the corner of the area where I was speaking. I let it run without focusing on anything in particular. This would usually yield a few minutes of decent material that I could turn into a clip for my website. Over time, I upgraded my clips as I spoke at larger events with professional recording services.

If you speak at such an event, arrange with the event organizer or the videographer to get a copy of any video and make sure you have permission to use it on your site. You can also hire a videographer to attend one of your events and make your own clips.

(3) Bonus material for the audience

More people are using video within presentations these days, for example, using short videos to illustrate a point or provoke discussion. If you speak on a technical subject where showing a system tutorial might be useful, a video can be more effective than braving the vagaries of the conference wi-fi for a live demo.

When speaking on self-publishing, I have used recordings of the self-publishing systems themselves, either within the session or as bonus material on the download page. This allows me to control the environment as much as possible, so the tech won't go wrong, and it allows people to watch the video later in their own time.

(4) Testimonials

Written testimonials are easier to get, but video testimonials have a lot of social proof because they are so real. This is best done with a group that you have worked with for a whole day when you have established relationships and can ask for volunteers.

Make people feel at ease so that they're smiling and ask a few warm-up questions like "Who are you, and what do you do?" Then ask about what they thought about the day and what they learned, as well as commenting on you as a speaker.

(5) Marketing

Video marketing on YouTube can be effective content marketing for growing your audience and building your email list. Talk about the key aspects of your speaking topic, or provide other useful, entertaining, or inspirational content.

(6) Premium courses for sale on your website

You can teach in greater depth through video, either through 'talking head' segments on your topic or through screen capture software if your niche is more technical. I create premium video courses for authors, and you can find more detail on this in chapter 3.14 on increasing your revenue streams.

Types of video and how to make them

There are many options for video creation. Here are just some examples:

Talking heads

This can be you alone at a specific location or at your computer. You can also video someone else in a live interview. You don't need to invest in any new gear to get started, just use your smartphone camera, but the sky's the limit if you love gadgets!

As an example, check out my video on how to find and work with professional editors at TheCreativePenn.com/editingtips

Online interview

I have hundreds of podcast interviews from Skype video on my YouTube channel, which I repurpose as audio for my podcast. It's a really cheap way to capture video, and most people are used to using Skype.

Use your computer webcam or buy a standalone webcam for under $100. You can use automatic recording software like Ecamm for Mac and Pamela for PC to record the raw video for editing later. You can also use Zoom or other video recording services.

Screen capture

This type of video is best for visuals on PowerPoint or Keynote or for recording your screen or software for tutorials or premium courses. You can use screen capture software like ScreenFlow for Mac or Camtasia for PC.

As an example, check out my tutorial video on how to use Vellum software to format your ebook and paperback at TheCreativePenn.com/vellum-tutorial

Time-lapse video

If you use your smartphone for video, there are all kinds of cool apps you can use. I used the TimeLapse app to create a video about book-binding, which might also be useful for other creative product demonstrations. You can see it at TheCreativePenn.com/bookbinding

Not all videos have to revolve around your speaking. They can just be for fun!

Social media video

Apps like Instagram, Facebook, and YouTube as well as new services that pop up all the time ,offer live video options. You can record live or create video from a montage of photos and clips to engage your audience further.

Editing your video

Most videos will need editing. You can start with free software that comes with most computers, either iMovie or MovieMaker, or use one of the many apps on your phone or tablet.

I use ScreenFlow on the Mac, which I also use for screen capture, so it is multi-purpose, but there are many options. Check out the recommendations online through reviews, and also watch YouTube videos on how to edit with the software so that you don't choose something too complicated or expensive for your needs. Remember to back up your raw video in case you want to change something later.

Distribution

I upload my marketing videos to YouTube. You can use the Unlisted or Private setting for videos you want to keep from the wider public.

You could also use Vimeo or other distributors who have different audiences as well as social media like Instagram and Facebook for short videos. Embed the video on your website, and people will be able to share it more easily.

Remember that copywriting rules and search engine optimization apply, so make sure that your videos have a compelling title and a good description that contain relevant keywords as well as appropriate tags for your niche.

You can check out my videos at:

YouTube.com/TheCreativePenn

3.12 Audio

As a speaker, your voice is a powerful tool for connection, but you can take this further, off the stage and into the digital world.

There will be many people who can't get to one of your live events, especially if you're marketing online to a global audience. But maybe they have a commute to work, or they're at the gym or doing chores, and are able to listen to you instead. The market for podcasts and audiobooks continues to grow, so even if you don't consume audio yourself, it's worth considering.

There are three main ways in which you can use audio:

(1) Downloadable audio from your site as a free giveaway

You can record and edit audio as an mp3 on free software like Audacity. You can install a player plugin on WordPress, or you can use a site like SoundCloud to embed audio on your site and make it easily shareable.

You could offer audio for free as a reason for people to subscribe to your email list or just as a bonus for your fans. I do this with an audio short story at JFPenn.com. You can also use it as the basis for a premium course, covered further in chapter 3.14 on increasing your revenue streams.

(2) Podcasting

Podcasting is audio (or video) that is distributed through online networks and podcast apps. It has exploded in popularity since 2016 based on the rise of streaming through smartphone networks, integrated into cars and in-home smart speakers like Alexa or Apple HomePod.

People can download the audio anytime and subscribe to their favorite shows, so they don't miss an installment which is downloaded automatically to their chosen device.

Podcasts can be talk shows, interviews, university lectures, stories, opinion pieces, or anything else you fancy. Hosting your own show can be a great way to build your credibility and audience within a niche which will lead to sales later, or you can pitch to appear on other people's shows to reach a wider audience.

I've been podcasting for over ten years with The Creative Penn Podcast, and I love the medium so much that I started another show, Books and Travel.

For more on how to podcast, check out:

TheCreativePenn.com/howtopodcast

(3) Audiobooks

Audiobooks are the fastest-growing segment in publishing and are a great way to reach readers with your message, especially in non-fiction niches as people are willing to spend money to improve their education and knowledge.

If you have a book, you can license your audio rights or use ACX.com or FindawayVoices.com to find partners to work with on production, narration, and distribution. You can also narrate, produce, and distribute your own audiobooks, as I do now.

For more on how to self-publish an audiobook, check out: TheCreativePenn.com/selfpublishaudio

3.13 How much to charge

"Remember to include a charge for your
preparation. Just because you happen to be
speaking on stage, you're not charging for 45 minutes.
**You're charging for all those years of experience,
all that preparation, all that practice."**

Clare Edwards, Brain-smart.com

The money question is always difficult, especially when you're starting out, but you need to tackle this head-on or you will never speak professionally.

How much you charge will depend on the following variables:

(1) Your audience and target market

If you're speaking for large corporates with big budgets on a valuable topic, you will be able to charge higher fees than if you're speaking on child-rearing to a group of parents at a local school, or on how to write a book to a group of writers.

It's not a judgment on your value or your expertise. It's more about how much money the target market is willing to pay. If you want to make a good income as a speaker, research your target market and look at the earning possibilities in that niche.

(2) The size of your platform and how in demand you are

Clearly, famous people can demand a higher speaking fee, but that can mean someone who is famous in a niche, so this is something you can aim for.

Alastair Humphreys is a well-known British adventurer and is paid accordingly in that market, but he wouldn't be in such demand if he was speaking about high-performance sales tactics because that is not his niche.

(3) Comparative speaker rates

There will always be other people who speak in your niche, so research what their rates are, then consider what differentiates you.

As creatives, we have an advantage, as we can also create original books and products that will help us be unique and stand out, even in a crowded market.

(4) The specific speaking opportunity and number of attendees

Keynote speeches at conferences with large numbers of attendees attract a higher rate than a small group talk.

You should also be paid more for a full-day than a half-day seminar or panel.

(5) The value of your information to the audience

You can charge more for a talk on how to trade stocks and shares successfully than you can for a sewing class, purely because people are willing to pay more when they can use the information to gain something in return.

"You're not trying to sell. You have something they want."

Clare Edwards, Brain-smart.com

(6) The value of the opportunity to you. How much do you want it?

Sometimes you will do things for free or lower your rates because of the possibilities that may arise afterward. For example, I spoke on Advanced Book Marketing at the London Book Fair a few years back. I did it happily for free because the opportunity was fantastic, and a number of the attendees signed up for my email list or bought my books or courses afterward. It also looks good on my speaking resumé.

Some speaking opportunities may offer a fixed payment, and you might be able to negotiate them upwards, or they might not be able to move on it. You'll have to weigh up the pros and cons based on how much you want the talk.

"My fees vary a lot according to the audience, who they are, where it is, how much of a hassle is it to get to, how enjoyable it might be, how useful it might be for networking, and how busy I am at the time."

Alastair Humphreys, adventurer

(7) Your attitude towards money

This is probably the most difficult aspect because we all have our own issues around money and self-worth. Try this exercise right now.

Look in a mirror and say, "My speaking rate is $1000 a day."

How does that feel? Did you choke on it or did it feel natural? Is it too high or too low?

Try saying different amounts out loud as if you were talking to someone who is asking you to speak. What feels like a worthwhile exchange of value for your time and experience?

Whatever you decide, re-evaluate it over time as you become a more experienced speaker.

Professional speaking is not a hobby

Speaking is an exchange of value, so both parties have to be happy with the deal.

The customer isn't paying for a 30-minute speech or a four-hour workshop. The customer is buying an experience, even a transformation. They are paying for the years of expertise that you bring to the session, as well as your preparation time and travel. This can amount to several days' work for even a short presentation.

If you're not happy with the rate on offer, feel free to negotiate. Include other products and services as part of the deal if appropriate, as the profit margin may be better than the speaker's fee. Always remember to charge travel and accommodation unless it's already included.

If the organizer is asking you to speak for free at a paid event, you should definitely negotiate, or consider whether this is the right opportunity for you.

> "In terms of pushing your rates upward, it really is about being **unique and delivering value** that no one else can easily replicate."
>
> *Mark McGuinness, WishfulThinking.co.uk*

When to say no to an opportunity

At some point, you will find that you have more than enough business, and you will need to evaluate and turn down some opportunities. This is where it's great to have a speaker network, as you can refer work to others, and this makes everybody happy.

Several factors go into the decision to say yes or no:

(1) Does this opportunity match the reasons why you're speaking?

Go back to the section at the beginning of the book on why you are speaking, and revisit your own reasons when considering whether to say yes.

As one of my goals for speaking is international travel, I will often take opportunities for lower fees that include travel expenses and the chance to visit somewhere new. For example, I once spoke at a five-day writer's retreat in Ubud, Bali, for little more than expenses only. But clearly, the trip itself was worth it!

(2) Is there a fair exchange of value?

The 'value' doesn't have to be financial. For example, speaking at the London Book Fair on the official program, an industry event where independent authors haven't really had much of a platform in the past, was worth it for me. Even though there was no financial payment, it was a step forward for indies, and the kudos on my speaker CV was worth it.

This would also be true of speaking at a conference that you want to attend anyway, where the speaker networking might be worth a lower fee or no payment at all.

(3) Does this opportunity fit into your personal goals and lifestyle?

Sometimes, you have to weigh everything up against lifestyle and what's really important.

For example, I was once asked to speak as the opening presenter and also to close a full-day conference in a city a few hours from where I live — on a Saturday. I had to be there early, leaving my house around 5 am and returning late that night. It would be a 15-16 hour day, and I would have to pay attention to the whole conference, which was not on a topic I would learn much from. The speaker's fee was tiny, and I would miss a whole day of the weekend with my husband. I turned that opportunity down.

> "You're going to start small. You're going to only just break even. You're going to lose time and money. But once people see that you're speaking from your heart, and you're delivering value, and you just keep giving and giving, something will happen. It really will."

Clare Edwards, Brain-smart.com

3.14 Increasing your revenue streams

When you run your own business, it's a good idea to create multiple streams of income, so you have more choice in your lifestyle and a buffer against changes in the industry. Here are some ideas.

(1) Speaking fees and repeat business

To be considered a professional speaker, you need to be making money from speaking, so charging a fee for services is important. But an event that goes well can often lead to other opportunities, so look for ways to work with the same client again.

After the speaker's fee is covered, you can address up-sell possibilities:

(2) Books, courses, and products sold 'at the back of the room'

Most professional speakers have books and physical or digital products available for sale at the back of the room. These products resonate with the theme of the talk, and if people are engaged with the presentation, they are likely to want more from you.

> If you need help with writing a book, check out my book, *How to Write Non-Fiction: Turn Your Knowledge into Words*.

As an introvert and creative, you're unlikely to want to do any kind of hard-sell, so all you need to do is have something else available. People will go find it themselves if they are interested.

(3) Books, courses or products sold from your website

Every time you speak, you will attract more people into your eco-system. If they are interested in you, they will come to your website and sign up for your email list and potentially browse what else you have to offer.

To encourage people to visit your website, remember to use a download page which provides further value to the audience, and a call to action for signup.

Once people are on your email list, you can market products, services, and other events later on. You can also make affiliate income this way, promoting books, products, and services that are not your own, but that you receive a commission on. I recommend that you only ever promote products or services that you use yourself and will be useful to your audience.

(4) Consulting or coaching

If your niche suits 1:1 consulting, you will likely find new clients through speaking. Make sure the audience knows it is an available option, by mentioning it when you speak, for example, "I was working with a client one day …" and ensure you have a clear page on your site with your offering.

These are just some examples of other forms of income. Here's some more detail on creating books and courses, in particular.

How to publish a book

Most professional speakers have at least one book that expands on the subject of their most popular talk, or around an idea they expect to develop into a speaking topic at some point.

If you're already an established speaker with an extensive platform, then you might get pitched by agents and publishers to write a book, or you can approach an agent or publisher directly. Always target those who have a track record in your niche.

The benefits of traditional publishing include the kudos and prestige of a publishing house, potential editorial and marketing support, and print distribution to bookstores. The drawbacks include a lack of control, a slow process to market and lower royalties as well as a lack of transparency around sales.

Many established speakers go the traditional publishing route as more of a marketing play and to use as a 'business card' in order to get higher speaking fees. It's not usually for the money.

Self-publishing, or being an independent (or indie) author, is increasingly the choice of those speakers who want to make money with their books, especially when they already have an audience to sell to.

The benefits of self-publishing include complete creative control over the book, pricing and marketing; faster speed to market and a higher royalty rate per book. The drawbacks include difficulty in print distribution to physical bookstores, the upfront budget required and, for some, a perceived stigma which has become almost non-existent in markets where online book purchases are significant like the US, UK, Australia, and Canada. After all, you can't tell an indie book if it has been edited and produced in a professional manner.

As a speaker, if you self-publish, you can make more money on print sales if you do your own print runs.

If you're interested in self-publishing, check out *Successful Self-Publishing: How to Self-Publish an Ebook, Print Book and Audiobook.*

How to create an online course

Online courses are fantastic because:

- They're **scalable**: you create them once, and they sell multiple times

- They target visual and audio learners so you can **reach more people** with your message

- You can reach people **globally** through the internet

- People will pay more for video and audio material, as it is perceived as **higher value**, even if the content is the same as your book

- With online tools these days, you don't need a great deal of technical skill, and the **profit margin can be significant**

What should your online course be about?

In order to maximize the chances of your speaking audience wanting to buy your course, it needs to be an extension of your talk, going more deeply into the topic.

So, I speak to writers and creative entrepreneurs, and I

have courses on *How to Write a Novel* and *How to Write Non-Fiction*, among other things.

Brainstorm ways your niche topic could be extended into an online course. From there, do some market research as to what other speakers are doing in that area.

Start with something small, for example, a short lecture for a low price or an online webinar. Is it a popular topic? Do people want to buy it? From there, you can build other modular courses or more premium level offerings.

Here's the process for creating an online course.

(1) Structure your course and create text-based material

If you have a book, you already have a structure, but you can also create a course even if you don't have a book on the topic.

Here are some other ways to get your material started:

(a) **Mindmap your ideas**, either on paper, or using FreeMind or other software if you prefer. This brainstorming will enable you to map out everything to include in the course; then you can turn this into a document and fill in the blanks with more detail.

(b) **Create a slide-pack** using PowerPoint or Keynote, or use one that you already have for a talk as the basis of the course. This is how I create the material for my own courses.

(c) **Record your speaking events** and get them transcribed. You may already have recordings, or you could record yourself talking about the various aspects of your material. Get this transcribed using a service like Trint.com or use speech-to-text software like Dragon, and you will have a document to use as a first draft.

(d) **Use Scrivener** to write and organize your material. I'm a huge fan of Scrivener and use it for all my writing.

You can now create a text PDF as the foundation for the multimedia aspects of your course.

(2) Produce video and audio content

As outlined in chapter 3.11, I record and edit video using Screenflow on the Mac. You can use Camtasia on a PC. I usually record myself talking to a slide-pack and also do technical screen capture videos, for example, how to use Scrivener to write a book.

You can also deliver your content through webinars using a service like GoToWebinar or Zoom, record the session and turn it into a mini-course.

(3) Choose a distribution platform

There are many options for hosting online these days that suit different levels of courses, for example, you could use Udemy for a free intro course or a cheaper version, and then sell your main offering through Teachable, which can manage payments and taxes as well as hosting and all the technical details.

You can use a custom install of WordPress with a separate theme and a membership plugin, but that takes time and effort to set up when there are so many hosted services these days. I used to do everything myself, but now I use and recommend Teachable.

Check them out at TheCreativePenn.com/teachable

Create a sales page listing the benefits to the customer as well as the price. You can offer discounts to your email list and audience to encourage them to purchase.

One tip is to get PayPal set up well in advance of any course launch as there are anti-fraud hoops you will need to navigate before PayPal lets you trade and transfer money to your bank account. But once it's sorted, it works really well.

As a speaker, you will be able to attract people to your courses through your talks, plus any marketing that you do for your speaking business will also bring traffic to your website, products, and services. Make sure that you have appropriate pages on your website for people to browse your products and courses.

You can find my courses at:

TheCreativePenn.com/courses

3.15 Financial considerations

The following chapter is not financial or legal advice. I am not a lawyer, an accountant, or a business advisor, so please consult a professional for your situation.

This is my own experience and opinion, so you know what to investigate further for your speaker business.

Contracts

If you're starting off small, a one-page agreement and an email from the event organizer are often enough to work from. But if you're moving into the big leagues, you'll need to consider proper contracts, deposit payments and more.

Always agree the speaker's fee and terms and conditions in advance and in writing. I usually forward this back to the organizer with my invoice, so they have evidence of what was agreed, especially if they book you well in advance or things change over time.

Some organizations will require you to sign a contract, so make sure that you read it carefully and change anything that isn't appropriate. I often print the contract off and hand-write any changes on it, as I initial each page.

They will likely ask for permission to record any sessions and to use your image in marketing. This is normal but just make sure it is specific to the event.

Insurance

The insurance that you need as a speaker will depend on the country in which you work, and also what kind of speaking you do. I'm pretty sure that Tony Robbins has some serious insurance for his fire-walking, but my intimate writer's event at the local arts center is not quite so risky!

Professional Indemnity and Public Liability Insurance were recommended when I worked in Australia. If you join a professional speakers' organization, this is something you can talk to them about and quite often get discounts and templates for, so I suggest that you investigate further especially if you are going to run your own events.

Invoicing

For most speaking events, you will need to invoice after the event. Make sure to do this in a timely manner, so you can get the payment process started as payment terms are often 30 days even if you request immediate payment.

Make a template invoice

All of the word processing and accounting packages have them. Use the template to create a personalized invoice per client that includes your speaker's fee and any expenses incurred. I usually keep a copy of the expenses and send the originals to the client if required.

The invoice should include your company name and number if you have one, any tax numbers and legal information, your company address as well as contact details, the amount and currency, a description of what you did, your bank details (or PayPal for some engagements), and when the payment is due.

Send the invoice to the client as soon as you have delivered on your contract

It's fine to send by email attachment. If you don't have an accounting system, and most speakers don't at the beginning of their career, print out the invoice and put it into a folder marked with the month when you expect it to be paid.

Set a reminder on your calendar to follow it up. You might expect bills to be paid promptly, but larger organizations, in particular, can be a nightmare. If you don't have a bookkeeper or accountant yet, make sure to go through your bank statements and check the incoming amounts for reconciliation. I've had some bills remain unpaid for over six months after an event, so it pays to be diligent in your follow-up.

Banking, tax, bookkeeping, and accounting

At the beginning of your speaking career, you may not have a business set up, and that's completely fine. You can start speaking as a sole trader (or whatever the term is in your country) and just add the income onto your tax return. But if you want to take things further, then at some point, you should discuss your business set up with a professional advisor.

It's a good idea to set up a separate bank account for your speaking work and, once you are more established, you may need an accountant for annual reports and taxation. In my second year of business, I also hired a part-time bookkeeper who does my receipts, account entry, and reconciliation, which is a huge help.

Don't leave these practical things too late, or you may get into trouble with cash flow.

The paperwork is just as important as the speaking for your business. You need to be a professional from beginning to end and look after your own business as well as your speaking development.

For more on business, check out my book, *Business for Authors: How to be an Author Entrepreneur.*

Conclusion and next steps

I hope that you've found some inspiration, comfort, and practical advice for your speaking career in this book. Now you've finished reading, I challenge you to take the next step, get out there and speak, even if it's just ten minutes at a local writing group to begin with.

Your speaking skills will improve with practice and time, so challenge yourself, say yes to opportunities and see where this adventure takes you.

Ten years ago, when I started speaking professionally, I was daunted by those who were years ahead of me in the game.

But time passes quickly, and now I've delivered professional speaking events all over the world. One of the things I love about the industry is the caliber of the people you meet, so I hope that you will join me on the journey.

Happy speaking adventures!

Thank you.
Need more help?

Thank you for joining me on your journey to public speaking. If you found the book useful, I'd really appreciate a review wherever you bought this or a share on social media. It really helps new readers discover the book!

Want to learn how to write, publish, and market your book?

Get your free Author 2.0 Blueprint and video series at TheCreativePenn.com/blueprint

Love audio?

Check out The Creative Penn Podcast on Apple Podcasts, Google Podcasts, and other podcast apps. Weekly interviews on writing, publishing, book marketing, and creative entrepreneurship.

Find the backlist at TheCreativePenn.com/podcast

My books are also available in audio format.

Find them all at TheCreativePenn.com/audio

Appendices

Appendix 1: Pre-speaking booking sheet

It's important to get this information over the phone, or by email prior to the event, and I sometimes email it to the client to make sure that we're in agreement.

Some events will have a contract, although many will not, and if you're doing any kind of travel, it's critical to have arrangements in writing.

You can download a Word document of this on the bonus page and modify this template to suit your own speaking engagements: TheCreativePenn.com/speakingdownload

Contact Name:

Contact Mobile:

Contact Email:

Date and time of event:

Time I am speaking within the event if not full day: *(for example, a slot within a conference)*

Venue address:

Title/theme for the overall event:

Title for my session:

Brief description: *(based on discussion with the client):*

Attendee Profile:

(Who are the audience, what do they want)

Pre-session questionnaire:

(If running a whole day session myself, I usually send out a questionnaire prior to the event in Google Docs so that I have more information about their questions. This isn't suitable for a conference, though.)

Agreed Speaking Fee/Deposit/Billing Terms:

Travel and accommodation arrangements and payment:

(For example, are they booking it all, or are you booking it and billing them later? I always prefer it if they pay for the travel and accommodation, in case of billing issues later.)

Books/Products - included as part of the package or permission to sell at the back of the room.

Handouts/Download page:

(I don't tend to do handouts unless specifically requested, but I do a download page for the slides and any extras, password-protected for the attendees only. If a handout is required, I will email a PDF prior for local printing.)

Feedback forms/process:

(Does the organizer do their own feedback form or can I use my own?)

Equipment required:

- Projector and screen
- Extension cord
- *(I usually take my own Mac, power cable and adaptor, but at conferences, you generally just provide the slides and use the organizer's computer).*
- Anything else

My contact details:

(Including any local information if traveling)

Appendix 2:
Speaking checklist

This is what I take with me to events. You can download a Word document of this on the bonus page to add to for your own engagements:

TheCreativePenn.com/speakingdownload

- Laptop and Mac adaptor

- Power cord and extension lead

- Slide clicker and spare batteries. I use an R800 Professional Presenter (wireless)

- A USB stick with your presentation in Keynote and PowerPoint format as well as PDF and handouts. I also make sure that these are on email as well just in case.

- Contact information for the venue in case of transportation issues

- Printout of slides

- Printout of bio/introduction if someone else is introducing you at the event

- Books and products for sale or a couple of examples if flying or if baggage weight is an issue

- Business cards

- Pens for flipcharts or whiteboard if appropriate

- Camera and/or video camera. It's always great to try and get photos of you in action, and you might not want to hand over your phone.

- Painkillers (just in case!)

- Bottle of water

Appendix 3: Questions for you to consider

These questions will help you to reflect on the content of the book, and answering them will enable you to prepare for your own speaking engagements.

You can download a Word document of this on the bonus page if you want to fill it in:

TheCreativePenn.com/speakingdownload

General questions

Why do I want to speak?

Where do I sit on the introversion/extroversion scale? What is my Myers-Briggs score?

PART 1: Practicalities of speaking

What type of speaking do I want to try? Is it instructional/ teaching or motivational?

What expertise do I already have? What am I passionate about?

How can I break those topics down into smaller, discrete chunks for various talks?

What are some of my key stories? What makes me unique? What is my message?

Who is my audience? Why do they want to know my story and my expertise?

Who will pay for this type of speaking?

Who are the other speakers in this niche? Who is already doing this?

What do I need to do in order to prepare for the event?

What do I need to do to manage my energy as a speaker?

How can I tailor my talk to this specific audience?

How can I make my slides amazing, if using them?

How do I want to communicate my brand through what I am wearing and my personal presentation?

What do I need to remember when I give the talk itself?

What do I want the audience to take away from the talk, in terms of closing message, as well as handouts or physical material?

How will I manage people during the session?

For a conference/panel, have I researched all of the other people involved and understood what I can bring that's different?

How will I handle feedback from the audience and the organizer?

How can I learn from the experience?

How will I improve my speaking over time?

PART 2: Mindset

How does speaking, or the thought of public speaking, make me feel right now?

What are the physical 'symptoms' of this anxiety? How can I reframe these feelings in a more positive way?

What are some examples of when I have faced anxiety and achieved something fantastic?

How can I prepare myself before events in order to manage this anxiety?

How can I grow my confidence in speaking?

What are the core aspects of my authentic self? What is it about me that is interesting, inspiring, or helpful for other people to know about that? How can I communicate that in my story?

PART 3: Practicalities of business

How will speaking fit into my existing business? Is it for income or for marketing purposes?

What methods will I use to get speaking work?

Will I run my own events, and if so, what do I need to make them successful?

How will I market my speaking?

How can I develop relationships with and work with other speakers?

What type of brand do I want to convey?

Have I set up a speaker's page on my website? Can I improve it?

Do I have a way for people to book me for speaking?

Do I have a professional photo to use in event promotion?

Do I have an email capture mechanism on my site?

How can I use content marketing to attract people to my business and speaker's page?

How can I use social media for marketing?

How can I incorporate multimedia into my website?

How much should I charge? How much are others in my niche charging?

What speaking opportunities do I want? What should I say no to?

How can I increase my revenue streams?

Am I managing the financial side of my business effectively?

Appendix 4:
Sales page example

This is a sales page example using EventBrite. Note that it specifically identifies the target audience as well as what they will learn (benefits), plus the expertise of the speaker.

Book Marketing Masterclass with Bestselling Authors Joanna Penn and Polly Courtney

<Date and time>

<Venue Address and map integration, included in Eventbrite>

A workshop for authors, led by two authors with years of marketing experience.

The first job of an author is, of course, to write great books, but these days, the second job is to market them.

Traditional publishers and agents want authors with marketing skills and a platform. If you're self-publishing, you definitely need to know how to do it yourself.

This full-day seminar is **for authors who want to sell more books**, but it's also for those writers who want to think more like an entrepreneur, even if they have only just started on the journey.

It's for traditionally published authors who want to take control of their future income, and for self-published authors who want to jump-start their sales. It's for fiction and non-fiction authors, with specific tips for both in the workshop.

What you will learn

- **Why marketing isn't scary**, discovering how your goals impact your marketing plans, and the strategies that don't change even when the online tools move on.

- **Your book fundamentals.** Understanding your target market, creating back blurb/sales copy, organizing your book page on the retail websites, including categories, pricing, and your tips for reaching the bestseller lists.

- How to get **book reviews** and use **paid advertising** for spiked sales.

- **Key aspects of traditional media and PR.** How to find the story about you and your book, how to choose and pitch editors and journalists, as well as how to act when you get the call. How to network in person and through professional speaking and events.

- **Your author platform, and marketing for the long-term.** Branding, your author website, email marketing, content marketing with text blogging, audio and video, plus social networking.

- Tips for **launching your book** and where to get started, as well as Q&A time with Polly and Joanna throughout the day

Learn from authors who specialize in marketing their own books

Joanna Penn writes bestselling thrillers under J.F.Penn and is also the author of non-fiction for writers, with over 500,000 books sold in 86 countries.

Joanna was voted one of The Guardian's Top 100 Creative Professionals in 2013, and her site for writers, TheCreativePenn.com has been voted one of the Top 10 Blogs for writers.

Joanna is an international professional speaker and has been featured on BBC World, Sky News, BBC Radio 4, The Guardian, The Independent, Forbes, London Book Fair, and Wired, although she focuses primarily on internet marketing. Connect with Joanna @thecreativepenn

"Joanna Penn has an intuitive understanding of how marketing works and how that pertains to the unique challenge of reaching readers and selling books. Her advice is always practical, actionable, and – most importantly of all – effective."

David Gaughran, author, *Let's Get Digital and Let's Get Visible*.

For more testimonials visit:

TheCreativePenn.com/testimonials

Polly Courtney is the author of six novels and a business book about entrepreneurship.

She is also an experienced speaker and media commentator with many TV, radio and press appearances including CNN, Channel 4 News, BBC News, Sky News, Grazia, Company Magazine, BBC Radio 4, Wired Magazine, The Independent, The Guardian, and Marie Claire.

In 2011, on the publication of her fifth novel, Courtney famously walked out on her publisher, HarperCollins, frustrated by the 'chick-lit' marketing of her books. Connect with Polly @pollycourtney

"Highly recommended. Polly clearly knew her stuff, presented all the information well and in a structured way. She was an engaging and encouraging speaker." "Very knowledgeable and very approachable."

Do you have questions about the Book Marketing Masterclass?

Contact Joanna Penn and Polly Courtney here. *[Insert contact info]*

Acknowledgments

For Jonathan.

Thank you for understanding my need to be alone, and being there when I'm ready to enter the world again.

I want to thank Susan Cain for her book, *Quiet*, which helped me finally embrace my introversion after many years of trying to hide beneath false extroversion. I'm also grateful to the NSAA in Brisbane for their training and support of a new speaker when I started out.

Huge thanks to my professional interview participants and fellow speakers:

Clare Edwards, professional speaker and author of *A Sprinkling of Magic. Brain-smart.com*

Alastair Humphreys, adventurer, professional speaker and author of *There Are Other Rivers* and other travel books. www.AlastairHumphreys.com

Mark McGuinness, poet, professional speaker, creative coach, and author of *Resilience*. www.WishfulThinking.co.uk and LateralAction.com

Thanks also to *Dan Holloway*, poet, author and publisher, for the chapter on performing your work. www.RogueInterrobang.com

Thanks to my publishing production team! To Jane Dixon Smith at JDSmith Design for rebooted cover and interior print formatting, and to Liz Broomfield at Libroediting for her proof-reading of the 1st edition.

Thanks to my Mum, Jacqui Penn, fellow introvert and my first reader, and to Kerry Howard, author, researcher and speaker at BletchleyParkResearch, for being a fantastic beta reader of the First Edition.

About Joanna Penn

Joanna Penn, writing as J.F.Penn, is an Award-nominated, New York Times and USA Today bestselling author of thrillers and dark fantasy, as well as writing inspirational non-fiction for authors.

She is an international professional speaker, podcaster, and award-winning entrepreneur. She lives in Bath, England with her husband and enjoys a nice G&T.

Joanna's award-winning site for writers, TheCreativePenn. com, helps people to write, publish and market their books through articles, audio, video and online products as well as live workshops.

Love thrillers? www.JFPenn.com
Love travel? www.BooksAndTravel.page

Connect with Joanna

www.TheCreativePenn.com
joanna@TheCreativePenn.com

www.twitter.com/thecreativepenn
www.facebook.com/TheCreativePenn
www.Instagram.com/jfpennauthor
www.youtube.com/thecreativepenn

More Books And Courses From Joanna Penn

Non-Fiction Books for Authors

How to Write Non-Fiction:
Turn Your Knowledge into Words

How to Market a Book

How to Make a Living with your Writing

Business for Authors: How to be an Author Entrepreneur

The Healthy Writer

Successful Self-Publishing

Co-writing a Book:
Collaboration and Co-creation for Writers

Public Speaking for Authors, Creatives
and Other Introverts

Career Change: Stop Hating your Job, Discover
What you Really Want to do and Start Doing it!

www.TheCreativePenn.com/books

Courses for authors

How to Write a Novel:
From Idea to First Draft to Finished Manuscript

How to Write Non-Fiction:
Turn your Knowledge into Words

Productivity for Authors

Content Marketing for Fiction Authors

www.TheCreativePenn.com/courses

Thriller novels as J.F.Penn

The ARKANE supernatural thriller series:

Stone of Fire #1
Crypt of Bone #2
Ark of Blood #3
One Day In Budapest #4
Day of the Vikings #5
Gates of Hell #6
One Day in New York #7
Destroyer of Worlds #8
End of Days #9
Valley of Dry Bones #10

If you like **crime thrillers with an
edge of the supernatural**, join Detective Jamie
Brooke and museum researcher Blake Daniel, in the
London Crime Thriller trilogy:

Desecration #1
Delirium #2
Deviance #3

The Mapwalker dark fantasy series

Map of Shadows #1
Map of Plagues #2

Risen Gods

American Demon Hunters: Sacrifice

A Thousand Fiendish Angels:
Short stories based on Dante's Inferno

The Dark Queen:
An Underwater Archaeology Short Story

More books coming soon.

You can sign up to be notified of new releases, giveaways
and pre-release specials - plus, get a free book!

www.JFPenn.com/free

Made in the USA
Las Vegas, NV
22 July 2024

92719769R00105